Trish Arnold

Trish Arnold

The Legacy of Her Movement Training for Actors

Lizzie Ballinger

methuen | drama

LONDON • NEW YORK • OXFORD • NEW DELHI • SYDNEY

METHUEN DRAMA
Bloomsbury Publishing Plc
50 Bedford Square, London, WC1B 3DP, UK
1385 Broadway, New York, NY 10018, USA
29 Earlsfort Terrace, Dublin 2, Ireland

BLOOMSBURY, METHUEN DRAMA and the Methuen Drama logo are trademarks of
Bloomsbury Publishing Plc

First published in Great Britain 2023

Cover design: Ben Anslow
Cover image © Ben John

A catalogue record for this book is available from the British Library.

A catalog record for this book is available from the Library of Congress.

ISBN: HB: 978-1-3502-6456-4
        PB: 978-1-3502-6455-7
        ePDF: 978-1-3502-6457-1
        eBook: 978-1-3502-6458-8

Typeset by RefineCatch Limited, Bungay, Suffolk
Printed and bound in Great Britain

To find out more about our authors and books visit www.bloomsbury.com
and sign up for our newsletters.

Contents

Acknowledgements

Trish Arnold died before she could see this finished work but she knew of its development and was able to offer her blessing and guidance on the early sections. I wish she had lived to hold it in her hands and smell the pages; to have finally seen her movements in a structured collation and her work given the recognition it deserves. This book is my 'thank you' to Trish Arnold, for developing a body of work that has touched so many and continues to influence actors, movement practitioners, directors and voice teachers around the world. Thank you to Sonia Olsen, Trish's daughter, for bestowing me with Trish's archive and allowing this book to develop.

A heartfelt thank you must go to Jane Gibson for passing on her knowledge and understanding of movement for actors. She was an inspirational mentor and gave me the opportunity to explore and evolve as a teacher and a person, for which I will always be grateful. And for her empathy and guidance. She continues to be a huge support.

I am indebted to Merry Conway for offering her wisdom and generosity. She has willingly given so much of her time towards this project, challenging and supporting me and my writing. Her sensitivity, thoughtfulness and curiosity has helped me to gather my thoughts and find clarity and confidence in my voice. I could not have finalized this book without her help.

A special thank you to Wendy Allnutt who spotted my potential; as my first mentor on this journey, her teaching and support was invaluable when I was starting out in my new career.

My thanks to the then Principal, Joanna Reed, and Head of Drama, Rodney Cottier, at LAMDA during my eight years of employment. They were both instrumental in enabling the mentorship with Jane Gibson to happen. And my thanks to John Baxter for supporting my teaching as Head of Movement at LAMDA during this time, and for his continued support as a friend and colleague. My thanks to LAMDA for funding and supporting the mentorship, and all those involved at the time, especially Anthony Quinn, for making this book possible from its beginning as a research project.

Thank you to all the movement practitioners that have taught me, influenced my journey and offered so much to so many actors and artists during their careers, for your passion and commitment, for insisting on the expressive body.

And thank you to those who have contributed to the writing of this book, who have offered their words and their time; Jane Gibson, Wendy Allnutt, Kristin Linklater, Declan Donnellan, Grace Olinski, Merry Conway, Florence Dobson, Sue Lefton, Samuel Tracy, Brad Cook, Beth Aylesbury, Eric Sirikian, Stephanie Arsoska, Eduardo Ackerman, Daniel Bowerbank, Lewis Merrylees, Olivia Nakintu, Melanie Joyce Bermudez and Francis Lovell.

A big thank you to Robyn Butler who was the inspiration for the design of the book, and to Ben John for the artwork scattered through the pages. Thanks to both my children, Daniel and Agatha, and my sisters, Rachel Jones and Harriet Jones, and sister-in-law, Flor Espinoza Jones, who helped out right at the end when the pressure was mounting. And thanks to my mum, Dinah Ballinger, who has always supported my journey into the arts where others had doubted.

Thank you to Patricia Pires Boulhosa and Christopher Burlinson for their brilliant editorial guidance. Thanks to Eliot Shrimpton for his help with editing.

Thanks to my editor, Anna Brewer, and assistant editor, Aanchal Vij, at Bloomsbury. Thanks to RADA for granting my sabbatical, and Alec at Pendred Printers. And thanks to Lesley Davies-Eldridge and Anna Brownsted.

And I couldn't begin to thank my partner, Adam Hurst, enough, for being by my side, for enabling me to write this book and supporting me through it from the beginning to the end. I have learnt and continue to learn so much from him.

This book is for the preservation of creative processes that take their time. For the importance of sensuality, specificity and sincerity, and of committing to a rigorous training that insists on these three things.

And it is also for my Dad.

Trish Arnold, left, Jane Gibson, right, 2008. Courtesy Jane Gibson, personal archive.

Foreword

When I met Trish for the first time in her tiny flat in Chiltern Street, little did I know it was to be the beginning of my career as a movement teacher and subsequently *Movement Director.*

As Head of Movement at LAMDA, Trish was looking for a good candidate to share the work. She asked me to show her something I would do to warm up the actors. As I remember, I rolled down the spine and then unrolled back up again! Trish was satisfied and I began my long apprenticeship with her as her student teacher.

I learnt so much.

The emphasis was on Movement specifically for actors with their need to speak! This was pioneering work that Trish had developed and was continuing to develop through all my time with her. The following archive of her work in sketches and notes will give an accurate account of this unique work.

She inspired me, let this book inspire you.

Jane Gibson
Movement Director and Choreographer

Introduction

I walk into the room. In front of me a group of actors are ready and waiting. I come to stillness with balance through my body and I ask them to find length through the spine; to focus on energy travelling upwards towards the sky, and down into the earth beneath their feet. There is a moment or two of silence for us to feel the natural flow of breath dropping in and out without effort. The silence allows the actors space to recognize how they feel and what they have brought into the room. It is an acknowledgement of the shared space and the journey we are about to go on. Yes, I am the guide, the tutor in the room, but we are in it together. If creative and exploratory things are to happen in this space, we need to be willing to offer and receive, ready to risk, to fall, to laugh and to cry, to make mistakes without judgement and discover the expressivity through our bodies.

Through a sequence of movements, I take the students on a journey that lasts an hour and a half. It begins slowly, with specificity and sensuality, and builds dynamically moment by moment as their bodies open and soften. They begin to connect deeply to their spines and awaken their desires. A little more attention is placed on breath and space. As the body becomes more flexible and fluid, the expressivity grows. An uncluttered and honest ability to listen and respond to the actor's own impulses (or those offered to them) reveals itself. The movements become bolder and riskier. They demand a stronger relationship to weight, breath and unforced sound. I witness the instruments, their body, becoming more three dimensional and dynamic, their imagination opening to all possibilities. As the space they inhabit becomes more vibrant and alive with creativity, I take a step back and observe their play, knowing the work contains them. We are part of the ever-shifting relationship between technique and expression, structure and free flow, order and chaos. They are speaking through their bodies with the possibility of language on their lips and the desire to speak burning deeply within. Often a word springs out and communication extends from the body to the voice. The journey always ends as we began, by coming back to stillness and silence. It is a reflective moment to absorb what has just happened and listen to what has been awakened.

I am a teacher of movement for actors and it is the practice known as Pure Movement that enables this journey to happen. At the core of my teaching is an understanding of the body's instinctive, dramatic capability and of how to encourage actors to use it to their full potential. My work is predominately within drama schools, now solely at RADA, where I have taught for several years and at present lead the Movement Department. I am also a Movement Director and run a private practice, an eclectic mix of leading workshops, mentoring the next generation of movement practitioners and offering one-to-one teaching for professionals from a range of backgrounds both inside and outside the arts.

For me, the body is at the centre of everything. Sixteen years ago I stepped into this practice. Coming from an actor's perspective and in need of redirection in my life, having worked in psychiatry for several years, I chose to train as a movement teacher. In those sixteen years I have been taught by many wonderful and inspiring practitioners, all of whom have left their mark on my own work. My teaching has evolved and will continue to evolve, but what I am certain about is that the work works. How? Because this training affects people, touches their spirit and shifts their perspective on the body as a creative instrument. It unveils a confidence that they can exist as an expressive and sensual being. Commit to the work, continue the exploration for a considerable amount of time and good things happen, whether you like it or not. The body becomes a powerful presence in the craft of acting and in life, where thoughts and feelings, intentions and impulses radiate out through the body, supporting language, gesture and the art of storytelling.

Pure Movement is a thoughtful and embodied practice that enables clarity of expression and creative intention. My aim over the course of a two- or three-year training is to equip actors with a craft they can take into any rehearsal room on any job. Through weekly or twice-weekly classes, for three terms per year, I teach actors a body of movements that speaks firstly to alignment and organization, then flows seamlessly towards greater expressivity. A profound relationship with gravity runs through this work, and actors discover the dramatic potential of the weight of their body through release. They complete their training with an inherent desire to work with the totality of themselves and bring the fullness of their physical instrument to all they do as artists; the body is not left behind as an afterthought in the craft of acting, but is at the forefront of everything.

Yet this journey involves a process of undoing that can be challenging at times. Coming into awareness of physical patterns and disconnections that previously have been necessary can be revealing. We all inhabit our bodies in varying ways and there is often good reason why we are drawn towards a disconnection. Our bodies hold the stories of our lives and it is natural to develop myriad defences to protect and survive. These manifest in a broad range of tensions, collapses or stresses. It can be hard to overcome these defences, even to question them, because they feel safe. Yet being able to choose other options may be exhilarating for the actor. The majority of our communication is through the body, with tone of voice and chosen words in second and third place – let's not choose to neglect the expressive possibilities and undervalue the power of our physical language.

In Pure Movement, technique and expression interweave in each other's strengths, for how can one exist without the other in acting? I see and feel for myself the freedom one can find through a containing and supportive structure. I witness many actors arriving with an understandable fear of opening out and revealing something of themselves, and year after year I watch them blossom into a place of sensuality, of physical and imaginative freedom, where they are willing and able to challenge themselves and support others. This practice holds them, contains them and allows them to risk. It helps them to develop a willingness to face, reflect and share one's own vulnerability and contradictions with an audience. And while its purpose is to train actors, it also provides me with a space to channel my own desire to creatively explore the wealth of human expression.

Pure Movement began with Trish Arnold, the pioneer of this movement training for actors. She developed a three-year training that began with alignment and release, and journeyed towards full and dynamic expressivity, a training that continues to influence and support actors around the globe. It has not been branded or codified and until now it has not been written down in its entirety. The practice has been passed on through body to body by virtue of a long-standing tradition of one-to-one teaching between movement practitioners.

What follows is a book of four parts. Chapter One tells of my encounter with Trish Arnold and the story of her professional life. With a prolific career across the globe in actor training and theatre, Trish insisted that to teach Pure Movement, the work must be first understood and embodied through mentorship and apprenticeship. In her wake she has left many brilliant practitioners, touched by her generosity and talent. Chapter Two is a self-reflective account of my mentorship with Movement Director and Choreographer Jane Gibson, detailing my development as a teacher of Pure Movement. Jane began her career as a student teacher under Trish Arnold in the 1970s and worked alongside Trish for many years. She continued the tradition of passing on the movement practice and as her first mentee I received the work through detailed and in-depth one-to-one training. Chapter Three is a collation of Trish Arnold's fundamental movements, arranged in a simple framework, with clear explanations of how to carry out each movement. It documents a lifetime of work for others to explore and enjoy. I have worked to honour Trish Arnold's vision and, when possible, I have her voice running alongside the descriptions taken from her notes and sketches. These explanations are marked by my own experience of Jane Gibson's teaching, an acknowledgement of the flow and evolution of the practice through three generations of movement teachers. The previous details of the mentorship may guide the reader when physically exploring the movements, encouraging specificity, sensuality and an ever-present relationship to weight, space and expression. Chapter Four offers the reader a collection of interviews, comments and writings from a variety of voices engaging with the movement work today – from actors in training who are fully immersed in the work to those recently graduated and taking the training on their professional journeys, and from directors who work with Jane Gibson to movement practitioners now being mentored by me. It provides a sense of continuation, the possibilities yet to come, and the necessary adaptions and evolution of the work.

The expressivity of Pure Movement cannot be easily translated through the written word, for the work is, of course, about embodiment. I have enlisted the help of an artist, Ben John, who has sketched several movements as he witnessed them in full flow. He has captured the weight of the body, the expression of a moment, the direction of a desire, an impulse. There are glimpses of a body moving in space, reflecting the possibility of individual discovery in the movement work itself.

This practice touches the spirit. I hope this book inspires others to search out opportunities to explore the world of movement training for actors, and to begin their own journey with Pure Movement.

One

Trish Arnold

———

*A Pioneer of Movement
Training for Actors*

TRISH ARNOLD

The actor needs to have at their disposal an instrument which will at all times express their dramatic intention.

The 'instrument' above consists of both the voice and body. My area is the actor's physical training but it must never be overlooked that one cannot function without the other.

So the first priority is to release physical tensions and free the breath. Only then will it be possible for the actor's imagination and invention to be matched with their ability to express it with body and voice. The aim of the movement training is to free and strengthen the student's body, to enliven the creative imagination, to enable the student to create a character's physical life and to give the student a range of specialised skills.[1]

Meeting Trish Arnold

My first encounter with Trish Arnold was in the autumn of 2006. I was to start individual sessions with her as part of an early module for my Masters Degree in movement training for actors at Guildhall School of Music and Drama. As I walked along Kilburn High Street towards her flat, I felt a heady mixture of excitement and trepidation. I had very recently jumped into this 'River of Movement' (as Trish used to call it); a practice I knew very little about, one that was intrinsically and quietly involved in global drama school training, theatre and film. It seemed to be a movement teaching that only a few practitioners worked with, a small family of sorts, where the work had been passed on from body to body. And I was heading towards the home of the founder, to meet the 'Godmother' of this movement work for the first time.

----

[1] Throughout this book, all uncredited quotes in italics are by Trish Arnold. Arnold's words, titles of exercises, and notes are quoted from my Masters thesis, *The Work of Trish Arnold* (unpublished Master thesis, Guildhall School of Music and Drama, 2008). This book is partially based on my Masters thesis.

Trish Arnold, *c.* 2015. Courtesy author's personal archive.

The woman that greeted me at the door was petite, elderly in appearance, yet had about her a strong and stable presence. There was warmth mingled with a directness and practicality, an openness that was immediately palpable. What struck me the most was her uprightness, a spine that remained at its full length and breadth, despite the unavoidable influence of age. As most shrink, collapse, fold inwards, Trish Arnold seemed to defy gravity and remained utterly connected to her spine.

She led me through to her flat.

> *Place your jacket and bag down in my bedroom somewhere, change if you need to, and we'll have some coffee after we've worked.*

Wonderfully welcoming while exuding authority and efficiency. We chatted briefly about the work, my background, then sprang into the practical. I was instructed to move the rocking chair, roll up the rug and begin.

A bounce
a swing
a stretch
a desire
an impulse
a moment of pure expression.
An adjustment, an explanation, a direction jotted down.

And so it continued, once a week. There was always the same welcome at the door, the same routine of furniture arranging and the same structure to our exploration, followed by the sharing of a small cafetière and warm milk. Yet the discoveries were never the same. I treasured these sessions with Trish. It was inspiring to be in the presence of her wisdom and passion for movement. Her knowledge of physical expression felt embodied, owned and trusted, and was being generously shared. I learnt that through a combination of hard work and an undeniable instinct for movement, she had had a full and vibrant career across the globe. Yet she had chosen not to codify or brand her practice. Instead, Trish had put her focus into the movements, their purpose for the actor and the passing on of the teaching. She radiated an air of clarity and silent insistence, as if there were no question she was in this world with the sole intention of developing this work. There was also a directness in Trish Arnold's communication, her teaching frank and sincere, and it kept me alert and willing to commit without wanting to please. The safe, homely space contained my newly discovered physical expression. I was being encouraged to connect deep into my body, my spine, to explore the movements and learn their origins. It was a captivating entry into this new world of movement training for actors. All from the front room of a flat in Kilburn.

During these sessions with Trish, I would watch her sieve through pages and pages of notes collected over the years, exercises written on the back of envelopes, scraps of paper, some printed on a typewriter. These apparent scribbles were often highlighted with wonderful doodles of stick people, next to proposals for movements hurriedly scrawled on the back of receipts, and sheets of lesson plans written in what can only be described as a foreign language to me at the time: 'cobra', 'animal drinking', 'Pluto under fence' and 'elephant swing', to name but a few of the titles given to specific exercises. It was then that I offered to assemble her notes into some sort of ordered fashion that could one day be considered a collection of work (and serve as a dissertation for my Masters Degree). I would collate and archive her movement training for actors. Trish Arnold gladly accepted this offer.

I continued to visit Trish regularly after my studies and act as an assistant for her when she taught other MA students after me. We would talk about the work, about her life. She kindly donated her books to me, those written by Michel Saint-Denis, Meyerhold, Litz Pisk, Craig, Lecoq, each one signed and dated by her as a reminder of a time and place. I would listen to the stories of her past, her journey from classical to modern dance, to movement for actors. She would talk with a genuine and deep respect for those who taught and influenced her throughout her life, and with a professional regard and tenderness for all those she had taught herself, her lineage deeply embedded in the passing on of her practice through one-to-one teaching. We would undoubtedly end up moving the rocking chair and rolling up the rug and she would direct me through her movements, adjusting me when necessary; tiny shifts in weight, in direction, in alignment, always insisting on the release of weight to enable expression and breath to flow freely. Every time I left her flat I was touched a little more deeply by the roots of her inspiration and philosophy, the movements dropping in to my body and spirit.

In the years that followed, as Trish was heading towards her mid-90s, I would often arrive at her flat with a pre-ordered quiche for lunch and a bunch of flowers, to find her swaying to her favourite Viennese Waltz. '*I'm practising balance*', she would say, determined to withhold the inevitable for as long as she could. It never ceased to amaze me how physically capable Trish was, how able to stand, with a hand on my shoulder or the edge of the sofa and swing her leg or reach up into the air. There was a beautiful simplicity to her gestures and movements, the expression radiated from deep inside and flowed out into space. She was an elderly woman and frailty was beginning to take hold, her balance eventually beginning to leave her (much to her utter frustration), but her movements, when demonstrated, had elegance and honesty, as if thought, breath, body and imagination were all working in one finely-tuned moment, entirely connected to each other.

**Trish Arnold with her children Sonia and Peter, 1950. Courtesy
Sonia Olsen, personal archive.**

The career

Trish Arnold was born 19 June 1918, in Peebles, on the Scottish Boarders. She was home schooled in Scotland and began her career in the 1930s as a classical ballet dancer, training at Sadlers Wells Ballet School, going on to perform with the Royal Ballet Company amongst others. After marrying and having her two children, Trish began teaching ballet but quickly became frustrated by the restraints of this traditional form and tired of the classical style of dance. Through friends she met a German dancer called Sigurd Leeder, an encounter that was to dramatically shape the direction of Trish's career. Leeder was a dancer, choreographer and teacher. His long-standing collaboration with the choreographer Kurt Jooss revolutionised modern dance in the 1920s and 1930s. Leeder and Jooss had developed Laban's work for dancers in their Modern Ballet. Together they most famously created the piece of work entitled *The Green Table*,[2] and it was Leeder who codified Jooss's work. Trish told me one afternoon in her flat that '*Kurt Jooss revolutionised ballet with his use of space and extension*',

When Trish met Leeder in the 1950s he was running his own school, named the Modern Dance Studio, in London. Trish joined his company for two years and it was there that her work shifted from classical ballet to the more modern forms of dance.

> *Sigurd Leeder's work centred around swings and space; it was very quick footed movements.*

Trish found herself deeply enamoured by Leeder's work; his dance style focused on space both in and around the body and the dynamic of free-flowing movement through swings. Leeder's dancing communicated human conflicts and integrated honest impulses, and it became an integral part of Trish's future. Through him she began a long relationship with the natural weight of the body and how this gives way to physical and emotional release, a stark contrast to the bound form of classical ballet. Leeder worked with a theatricality that spoke to Trish and helped guide her into movement for theatre.

Approached by the London School of Music and Dramatic Art (LAMDA) in the mid-1950s, Trish was invited to teach movement for actors, to develop her use of modern dance to suit actor training. She willingly joined the principal at the time, Michael MacOwan, vice-principal Norman Ayrton and the voice coach, Iris Warren, all of whom were instrumental in Trish Arnold's development as an expert in the field of movement for actors.

---

[2] *The Green Table*, choreographed by Kurt Jooss, first performed for the 'Concours international de chorégraphie en souvenir de Jean Borlin', organised by the Archives Internationales de la Danse, Théâtre des Champs-Elysées, Paris, 3 July 1932.

> *Turning around from Leeder and coming face to face with Iris Warren, Trish made huge changes and adaptions.*
>
> **Merry Conway**[3]

It was here at LAMDA that Trish began to pioneer a body of work centred around weight and the dynamic use of swings while integrating the actor's need to breathe and speak. Trish Arnold described herself as *'having been greatly influenced by the powerful voice coach, Iris Warren.'* Trish was discovering the fundamental differences between the needs of an actor and those of a dancer.

> *The first time I met her* [Iris Warren] *she rose up to full height and said 'And I hope you're not going to do anything that stops them breathing!'*

With this powerful combination of practitioners:

> *LAMDA was at the time creating a school that was in many ways a reaction to Noel Coward and a style of acting that had existed for many decades. They were trying to create new actors.*
>
> **Merry Conway**

Trish Arnold redesigned the approach to British movement training for actors, one that worked alongside the traditions of fight and dance as physical and theatrical education but connected the disciplines together, enabling the body to support the actor's creative intention and to communicate with sincerity, with impulse. And to support the voice. Trish was eventually made Head of Movement at LAMDA and remained in this position from 1963 to 1974, incorporating a movement teaching that connected with weight, breath, space and humanity into the fabric of LAMDA's actor training.

> *Trish used to talk to me about actors turning up to movement classes at LAMDA in suits. Her thing was to develop a programme, redefine it. She didn't codify the work, she lived it. She saw what was in front of her. She observed and saw what was needed and took what she knew about the body*

---

[3]Merry Conway is an American movement practitioner, creator, and mentee of Trish Arnold. She directed and produced the film *Tea With Trish*, 2008; a documentary detailing the work of Trish Arnold.

and aligned it with the voice. She integrated it into a whole three-year programme that took an actor from alignment to full expressivity.

Merry Conway

It was also at LAMDA that Trish Arnold became aware of the work of the French teacher and director, Michel Saint-Denis. Michael MacOwan and Norman Aryton had both previously worked with Saint-Denis and were determined to continue his unique and revolutionary style of actor training. Michel Saint-Denis had inspired many artists during his time at the London Theatre Studio, before the Second World War, and afterwards at the Old Vic School with his own actor training that involved movement, improvisation and mask work. It was the acting principles of Michel Saint-Denis that fed Trish's desire to further her own education and to study with Jacques Lecoq in Paris. Lecoq was also a huge influence and enabled Trish to link the purer aspects of the movement teaching into movement improvisation. She began to teach mask work and animal studies and to engage with many of Lecoq's principles for dramatic exploration through the body. Another inspiring movement practitioner that deeply affected Trish Arnold's development in movement training was Litz Pisk. At the time, Litz was also revolutionising movement for actors, both in drama schools and the theatre, insisting on meaning through movement to free the actor's body.

Jane Gibson: the student teacher

It was in the 1970s that Trish met a young actress named Jane Gibson. Celia Gore Booth, an actress who had trained at LAMDA and had met Jane at the Lecoq school in Paris, recommended her as a possible movement person to Norman Ayrton, following his appointment as principal of LAMDA. He interviewed Jane, and subsequently asked Trish as Head of Movement to meet her too. Trish immediately observed that Jane had an undeniable instinct for movement, much like herself. And so began Jane's work at LAMDA, learning the art of teaching Trish's movement practice for actors. She learnt:

What to teach and how to teach it! Classes of students were split into two groups. I would participate in the first class and notate the next one. I did this for many years. I started to teach alongside Trish in a studio space that she could oversee from her class. (I was in a garden studio.) Mostly she would shake her head sadly at what she saw! 'Too many things' she would tell me afterwards. Trish had an accuracy and a specificity that was extraordinary. I had to acquire that too.

Jane Gibson

Jane Gibson continued to teach with Trish at LAMDA for several years before taking the work from drama schools into the acting profession. She went on to become one of the country's most renowned Movement Directors. Trish Arnold supported and accepted Jane's development of her own style of movement, and as she moved away from teaching, she could see that Jane's practice was full of her own vision.

Trish never had an injury in all her life, I have never known her to injure herself, that's good use, she never pushed, she knew her body.

Jane Gibson

Trish Arnold, second right, date unknown. Courtesy author's personal archive.

Trish went on to offer her time and knowledge to several other people throughout her career, continuing the tradition of passing on an embodied practice. Many who were drawn to Trish's work already had established careers but were keen to learn what Trish Arnold had to offer, knowing that her work would enhance what they already knew and deepen their own practice. Alongside Jane Gibson were Wendy Allnutt, Sue Lefton, Shona Morris and Jackie Snow, to name a few, all UK-based teachers, actors, dancers, gymnasts who experienced Trish Arnold's detailed teaching. Across the sea, as Trish's career became global and her time shared between the UK, America and Canada, she influenced Merry Conway, Susan Dibble and Kristin Wold among others.

> *She was so generous, open and accepting of the whole person and how they could be more of themselves. Rigorous in her opinions but she didn't want those she taught to be all the same.*

Merry Conway

Kristin Linklater: the collaboration

———————

Shortly into her time at LAMDA, Trish was regularly asked to work as Movement Director on various productions with the English Stage Society, under the direction of William Gaskill and Peter Gill. From 1967 to 1974 Trish Arnold was also employed as Movement Coach at the highly reputable Stratford Ontario Festival in Canada, working under Artistic Director Michael Langham. In Stratford, Ontario, Trish Arnold continued to build a close working relationship with the voice coach Kristin Linklater that was to last for many years. They first met at LAMDA when Kristin was training as an actor and was taught movement by Trish, and it was at LAMDA that they later became teaching colleagues. Kristin recalled the work at Stratford as '*band-aid stuff, patching and repairing actors' problems*', and these shortcomings led both Kristin and Trish to recognise that there was a greater need to integrate voice and movement work.

> *Michael MacOwan used to introduce us as 'Kristin Linklater, the voice, and Trish Arnold, the body!' Kristin used to say: 'There's a breath with every movement – you don't hold your breath to do a movement, you let your voice go out with a movement.'*

In 1968 Trish went to America to teach movement at New York University and worked with Kristin once again. Kristin further developed her work from the mid-1960s to 1978 and Trish participated in Kristin's innovative training school called *The Working Theater*, co-founded with acting teachers Peter Kass and Joe Chaikin. In 1977 she joined the faculty at Carnegie Mellon University as Head of Movement in the Drama Conservatory Program, where until 1980 she taught for the first half of the year, leaving the second half of the year for her American mentee, Merry Conway, to continue the work.

The following piece of writing by Kristin Linklater was kindly given to me a few months before she died. After I approached Kristin to ask whether she would like to say a few words about Trish for this book, I received this:

> *I went to LAMDA as an acting student when I was 18 – perhaps only 17 – Michael MacOwan, the principal of LAMDA, believed in taking students when they were as young as 16 so that they could be trained before they had developed bad habits. He created a serious drama school with some teachers drawn from the renowned, short-lived Old Vic Theatre School. His faculty included my teacher, Iris Warren, who had a prestigious private voice studio in Wigmore Street and had taught at the London Theatre Studio and, for movement, Norman Ayrton from the Old Vic Theatre School. Trish Arnold was the second movement teacher. I have only vague memories of her during my time as a student at LAMDA (perhaps she joined the faculty later) but when Michael MacOwan hired me to train and teach with Iris Warren in 1957 I began a collaboration with Trish that continued sporadically but vitally for several decades. Physical awareness and relaxation were essentials as a base for the voice work. Iris would have students lie on the floor to find their relaxed breathing and we would roll our heads and necks around to release throat tension but it was with Trish that we would drop down the spine and learn to recognise and follow physical impulses.*

> *My only really vivid memory of working as a fledgling teacher with Trish is of the two of us exploring ways of stimulating students into letting the imagery in words be the impulses that moved their bodies. Having discarded many poetic options we chose 'The Kraken' by Tennyson.*

Below the thunders of the upper deep,
Far, far beneath in the abysmal sea,
His ancient, dreamless, uninvaded sleep
The Kraken sleepeth: faintest sunlights flee
About his shadowy sides: above him swell
Huge sponges of millennial growth and height;
And far away into the sickly light,
From many a wondrous grot and secret cell
Unnumbered and enormous polypi
Winnow with giant arms the slumbering green.
There hath he lain for ages and will lie
Battening upon huge sea-worms in his sleep,
Until the latter fire shall heat the deep;
Then once by man and angels to be seen,
In roaring he shall rise and on the surface die.[4]

I remember the students rolling around the studio mumbling, intoning, vibrating with sumptuous abandon as they chanted:

'Unnumbered and enormous polypi
Winnow with giant arms the slumbering green.'

This, in retrospect, was the start of my Sound and Movement work which I developed in the 1970s in the States to bring Shakespeare's language out of the head and into the body. I started working with Shakespeare & Company in Lenox, Massachusetts, in 1978 and as we developed our 4-week intensive workshops we began to invite Trish regularly to teach movement and to train other teachers in what is now called Pure Movement. Her legacy lives on in the U.S. with Susan Dibble, Merry Conway, Kristin Wold and others.

It became clear that Trish's approach to freeing the actor's body was the essential physical companion to Freeing the Natural Voice. As long as she was able to travel I would bring Trish to the States for my voice teacher-training programmes. Her passionate interest never flagged and she never stopped exploring the minutiae of movement. And, yes, swings will always be trade-marked Trish Arnold in our world.

Kristin Linklater

---

[4] Alfred, Lord Tennyson, *Poems, Chiefly Lyrical.* Effingham Wilson, 1830.

**From left to right: Jane Gibson, Trish Arnold and Kristin Linklater, *c.* 2015,
Courtesy author's personal archive.**

Back in England, during the 1970s, Trish Arnold and Jane Gibson were heavily involved with Frank Whitten and Chattie Salaman in Common Stock Theatre, a theatrical movement committed to community theatre. Trish still travelled to America to teach movement at Shakespeare & Company, founded by Kristin Linklater and Tina Packer, often taking Jane Gibson with her as her assistant. Merry Conway also taught at the company some time later.

Trish passed her work to several other teachers at Shakespeare & Company, notably Susan Dibble, Karen Beaumont and Kristin Wold. She worked with several generations of voice teachers trained by Kristin Linklater in their rigorous training programme and Merry Conway continues the collaboration with the Kristin Linklater Voice Centre to date. In 1985 Trish Arnold began teaching at Guildhall School of Music and Drama where she met with the voice coach Patsy Rodenburg. She took the position of Head of Movement at Guildhall in 1989, continuing to train actors there until 1995. Following her retirement from Guildhall, Trish taught privately in London and has passed on her work to a younger generation of movement teachers including me.

> *Trish had an art of breaking down a movement; know what the 'final' is, then do it bit by bit ... don't talk too much. Keep instructions simple, if you talk too*

*much it becomes intellectual, too much in the head rather than about moving,
the movement in the body.*

Jane Gibson

Thoughts on movement

I once asked Trish if she could characterise her fundamental principles for movement training for actors; this is how she responded:

> *I teach what I think actors need! What they need to be able to work on stage.
> If they can't move, they can't act!*

She then proceeded to produce a dusty old pamphlet sealed in a plastic bag. This worn-out and obviously immensely treasured artefact was a short book written in French in 1942, entitled *Expression Corporelle du Commedian* by Jan Doat, a theatre director, writer, actor and teacher. She translated a few key sentences, declaring that her own philosophies were very similar to his and could be used to best describe her opinion on movement training for actors. Here is the opening paragraph:

> '*If one compares a play with a symphony, you can say that, under the director
> – the conductor in this case – the actor is both the instrumentalist and the
> instrument. He is an instrumentalist because he translates, through the use of
> his intelligence, his sensibility and his artistry, a written text, just as a musician
> translates his written score. He is an instrument because he can express his art
> with his voice, movement and the play of his body. When a man reveals a
> work of fiction to other men with the help of these three elements, it is theatre.*

Jan Doat[5]

The teachings of Jan Doat have not been so widely recognised but their influence is felt in the work of renowned French theatre director Jacques Copeau, founder of Théâtre du Vieux-Colombier, in the early twentieth century. Copeau's philosophies in turn

---

[5]Jan Doat, *L'expression corporelle du Comédien*, 3 ed. Paris: Éditions de L'amicale – Librarie Théâtrale, 1966, p. 7.

impacted on the work of his nephew, Michel Saint-Denis. There were many crossovers and collaborations from a European lineage that revolutionised theatre in the twentieth century, and as a consequence a new actor training developed, one that integrated body and voice as essential and fundamental aspects of all acting. This ethos is now embedded in our twenty-first-century understanding of actor training and continues to evolve. The Pure Movement 'river' also continues to flow and at the heart of the practice remains Trish Arnold's belief that movement training for actors is:

> *The teaching of truth, strength and beauty of corporal expression.*

Two

Body to Body

The Passing on of an Embodied Practice

My journey

My early years were filled with ballet, sports of all kinds and horses, in particular dressage. My desire for all things physical met with a passion for the theatre during my early teens and this led me to the pursuit of acting. As a spirited teenager, the theatre became an effective way to nurture my expressivity and explore the depths of my imagination. In the late 1990s I trained as an actor at Manchester Metropolitan University. The defining memory of my time at drama school was the joyous integration of body and voice and a training that was highly physical. It provided me with a strong foundation in the exploration of the expressive body.

For several years I worked as an actor in theatre, TV and film, drawn to devising projects and new writing that allowed me freedom to play and engage the totality of my creative self. In between acting roles I made a living as an auxiliary nurse on psychiatric wards in Manchester. I found myself more and more engrossed with this challenging job, and over time I realised I had stepped away from acting into the unsettling world of mental health. During these years working in acute psychiatry, I witnessed the fragility of the mind, the wondrous diversity of humanity and the remarkable capacity of humankind – at times it was deeply harrowing, the weight of humanity fully visible from the depths of despair to the utter joys of life. It was a place of unfiltered, raw and heightened expression where people articulated their emotions and experiences in unfettered and impulsive ways. I learnt many lessons during this experience that have stayed with me and continue to inform me.

After five years in psychiatry I turned back towards the theatre, hoping to make a deeper exploration into dramatic expression and to explore its possibilities outside performing. I had heard about a new Master of Arts teaching actors Movement or Voice at Guildhall School of Music and Drama, London, and applied. At the interview, the Head of Movement, Wendy Allnutt, noticed my physical ability; she speaks about how she came to offer me a place:

> *Lizzie Ballinger was amongst a small group of finalists to be interviewed for the then new MA in Actor Training specialising in either Voice or Movement. There was to be a small workshop of voice and movement in which all the candidates would take part before being interviewed. Only one participant*

was to be chosen to partake in each strand. Lizzie had applied for the vocal strand.

I was looking for someone with an understanding of drama, a strong healthy body and someone who would be sensitive in their approach to others.

As the workshop proceeded I found my eye constantly drawn to Lizzie. She executed a simple roll up the spine with sensitivity and accuracy, she lifted her arm when prompted as though spreading a golden cloak (a Trish Arnold description). When interviewed Lizzie told us that she had just won a kick boxing competition despite only just learning the skill and had also spent her summer mucking out horses. She had worked as a psychiatric nurse between acting jobs and that she no longer wanted to work as an actress but to specialise in voice. Imagine my disappointment, no one else in the group fulfilled the job description for the movement MA but Lizzie. She was obviously strong, had stamina and determination alongside the interactive skills of working sensitively with people.

In discussion with Diana Devlin (Head of Drama Studies) I decided not to take any of the other candidates, Lizzie had made such a strong impression that in the full knowledge that she would be disappointed not to be offered the Voice strand I decided to offer her a place as the Movement MA. She accepted.

Wendy Allnutt

I began at Guildhall in September 2006. It was the very first year of the new MA degree and I was the only movement teacher on the course. Specifically designed as a teaching course in Movement Training for Actors, it ran part-time over two years. Guildhall was addressing the need to educate and nurture more teachers in the particular areas of movement and voice training for actors. By adopting an apprenticeship-style structure to teach a specific practice, Guildhall chose not to follow a multi-discipline approach in training teachers, as other MA courses were doing. It was an experiential process of learning, centred around the pedagogy of Trish Arnold and Patsy Rodenburg, where information was not passed on through codification, or learnt through a textbook. It involved the act of doing and undoing, through observation and embodiment as a starting point. I followed first- and second-year students on the BA Acting Course, participating in a movement class and observing the next. I was also present in rehearsals of acting projects and final-year productions. The movement training at Guildhall at Guildhall for the BA Acting students was based on Trish Arnold's practice. I learnt how Pure Movement connected to every aspect of an actor's journey from alignment to full expressivity, through animal and mask work, historical and social dance, into voice work, acting projects and productions. And because of Wendy Allnutt's extraordinary ability to wed movement to acting, I developed a tangible understanding of how to bring an actor's imagination into the body, into every character and every given situation. Supported by the many discussions with Wendy, I started to understand the complete journey of the actor in training, using Pure Movement as a foundation for acting. What defined the Guildhall actor training at that time was an integrated approach to the actor's education, one that connected the body, voice and imagination directly to acting through all staff and all departments. I learnt as much as possible from the teachings of Patsy Rodenburg and discovered that Trish Arnold's movement work entirely connected with, and supported, Rodenburg's teaching of the free voice. It was at Guildhall that I reawakened my love of theatre and was delighted that my desire for physical expression could be channelled into a career path that nurtured many aspects of my life.

During my teacher training at Guildhall I, like all students, went through the process of imitation. I learnt the movements and imitated the teaching styles of my tutors, a necessary starting place as I had never taught before. After graduating I spent a few years finding my teacher's feet, rushing from one drama school to another, saying yes to everything. My journey as a movement practitioner had well and truly begun and my teaching skills developed with every job. My next significant encounter was to meet Jane Gibson, when my perception of Pure Movement changed significantly.

The mentorship with Jane Gibson

I have tried for a long time to find a way of recording what I have learnt during my mentorship with Jane Gibson. When I look back over the notebooks from my mentorship, I am moved by what I read because I am reminded of the many changes that happened in me. I remember where I was when I started and can acknowledge where I am now. It was a journey of self-discovery. As I expanded my ability to teach Pure Movement with the specificity, care and clarity that both Trish Arnold and Jane Gibson demanded, I also learnt about myself, growing into my body and mind, discovering my strengths and my individual creativity. Through this movement work I continued to carve out a deeper vessel for my expressivity, one that would hold and support my inner world and my creative desire. For the first time in my life I learnt to trust myself and to be proud of what I had to offer. This practice resonated with the deepest parts of me. I understood it and realised I was able to communicate it to other people.

My experiences during those three years of one-to-one work with Jane Gibson were transformative, even life-changing, yet at the time the evolution of my teaching often felt slow, barely noticeable, with small shifts that seemed to take a long time to happen. It is natural to resist change and this can make the challenging of habitual patterns a slow process. But how can my unfolding and growth be written about? How can something that is so embodied, so subtle and unspoken be put into words, and something so personal be brought into a public arena?

I first heard about Jane Gibson when I was studying at Guildhall. She was a powerful figure in this particular field of movement and was mentioned frequently during my training. People spoke about Jane Gibson's brilliance as a movement practitioner and her direct manner that matched a demanding and rigorous approach to movement for actors. Jane's journey into movement began through her mother, who was a qualified Scottish Country Dance teacher, and Jane was often taken to the many venues where she taught. Jane states:

> We were all (my father, brother and I) dragooned into dancing in the hall of
> the house we lived in.[1]

She went on to train as an actress at the Central School of Speech and Drama, London, where she was taught movement by the renowned Litz Pisk, followed by time in Paris training with Jacques Lecoq. As a young woman with a lived experience of dance and the actor's physicality, she went on to become a student teacher of movement under Trish Arnold at LAMDA. This was the beginning of Jane's adventure into teaching actor's movement, learning Trish's work through a one-to-one relationship that fed directly into her teaching. This apprenticeship allowed Jane the gift of time and space to fully absorb Trish Arnold's fresh and dynamic practice. After several years of teaching, Jane Gibson moved away from education and into movement directing for theatre, film and opera,

---

[1] In this chapter, all uncredited quotes in italics are by Jane Gibson.

utilising her knowledge of the body to serve a director's vision. As an Emmy Nominated Choreographer and Movement Director, Jane has a long résumé of work with prestigious theatre and opera companies such as RSC, ROH and the NT, and many film and TV credits. She remains the first and only Head of Movement at the National Theatre under Richard Eyre and is an Associate Director of Cheek By Jowl, having worked closely with Declan Donnellan for nearly thirty years. Jane continued her deep relationship with Trish Arnold as both friend and colleague in the many years that followed.

In 2012, after having taught for four years, I applied for a teaching position at LAMDA. I finally met Jane Gibson on the interview panel. Following the interview, LAMDA not only asked if I would teach for them but offered me a two-year mentorship with Jane Gibson, funded entirely by them – a progressive concept that was new to modern-day drama schools. This was a huge investment and an astonishing offer made under the perceptive leadership of Joanna Read, the Principal of LAMDA at the time. Burdened with financial pressures as are all drama schools, LAMDA was regardless prepared to invest in both the teaching and the teachers with seriousness, depth and money. The school wanted to support a tried-and-tested tradition of mentorship that involved intensive, embodied learning. It was an exciting opportunity for an institution to adopt the eye of someone who holds knowledge and employ them to pass this on to someone else, linking Trish's work at LAMDA in the past to a future training. Yet perhaps more importantly, the investment meant I could pass on that depth of knowledge, commitment and passion to all those I taught at LAMDA until I left in 2020, and onwards in my work ever since.

The mentorship would lead to profound changes in myself and my approach to teaching. Having briefly observed my teaching in the interview, Jane revealed her initial impressions to me sometime later – what she saw in my work was a competent teacher and an instinctive mover, someone with potential and a strong foundation in the teaching of Pure Movement; but she also found that my teaching was scattered, missing the essential flow, jumping from one movement into another with no clear progression.

You were all over the place but also rather good.

Based on her observations and her own experience as a student teacher, Jane organised the mentorship into three sections: content, structure and form. Through content, Jane wanted to expand my knowledge of the movement work and lead me to fully embody each individual movement. Structure focused on the journey of progression throughout each class, and subsequently my students' development across a two-year training. Through form, Jane wanted to connect all aspects of my learning to make me a less scattered, more grounded and confident teacher, to help me find more flow in my teaching with my own creativity at the forefront. She wanted me to find my own voice and dynamic, my own style of teaching, just as Trish had done for her. Jane was a young woman when she received her apprenticeship with Trish Arnold and she had experienced the joy of time to unpack the work. She now wanted to pass this on to me, allowing me to deepen and evolve my own practice and build on the journey I had already begun.

The mentorship ran over the course of three years, with various stop gaps for the birth of my second child and certain professional obligations requiring Jane's full commitment. It consisted of weekly one-to-one sessions in a studio at LAMDA. First, Jane demonstrated what she would like me to do and then she observed my exploration. She adjusted me where necessary, guiding me through the development of the movement work. In some weeks Jane sat quietly by as I taught a first- or second-year class, observing and taking notes. The following week those notes would be given to me and we discussed her feedback – moments when the journey of the class had faltered, for example, when my timing and creativity had stumbled, as well as the moments that flowed. I scribbled down these observations at speed and added my own thoughts and discoveries later on the train home.

I adored these sessions. What a joy to be a student again. I experienced the liberation of learning Pure Movement for an hour each week, without the pressures of teaching. I took a back seat from teaching and experienced a swing, the release, a stretch, all the while being led by someone else. Yes, I learnt how to teach the movements but first and foremost I learnt how to embody them. And I heard a new voice guiding me through the movements, Jane's voice, one that was shaped by Trish Arnold's early career and yet full of experience and wisdom in its own right. It was a different voice from my experiences at Guildhall where movement training was based on the whole spectrum of movement leading directly into acting. At Guildhall I had learnt from Wendy Allnutt, a successful actress who later moved into teaching. Wendy's practice had a strong connection to directing and blossomed out of Pure Movement. Her teaching had been hugely influenced by Trish's later practice that had naturally evolved from her LAMDA days. Wendy absorbed movement training from Trish, bringing her own creativity and flavour into the teaching, as did all those who had been touched by Trish Arnold's vision. This is what I was familiar with, this is what was in my body. Jane, however, focused entirely on the detail and expression within Pure Movement. When taught by Jane, the movements already familiar to me revealed a pedagogical specificity that I had not noticed before, details I had overlooked or been unable to acknowledge. During the mentorship I was ready and able to unpack them. The movements had slight variations, a weighted sense of precision and purity that was new to me, and a deep connection to desire.

From Jane I experienced movements that felt reflective of Trish's early days, when she was full of the vitality of a new career path and as she discovered and invented as she went. Trish had worked under Norman Ayrton and Michael MacOwan at LAMDA for the first few years and had immersed herself in a new world of movement for actors. She re-directed the movements of the dancer for the actor and, based on a new attention to breath and impulse, created a clarity of intention. Always present was the focus on how to find physical expressivity through the actor's body. Under the gaze of voice teacher Iris Warren, Trish worked to incorporate effortless breathing into the movements, following the body's impulses into sound. Jane's own holding of the work became clearer to me as well; alongside Trish, there were traces of the influence of Litz Pisk and Jacques Lecoq, emphasising a foundation for Jane's own evolution of the movement work around breath, suspension, expression and text.

These principles filtered into movements that were both new and familiar to me, helping me to build on my own content and develop my physical language. It was exciting to feel myself becoming more conscious, more critical of my own teaching; to gain size by coming into my body's full length and breadth and discovering my own inner strength. Jane's clarity of detail is a gift in her teaching and comes as a result of her own time spent exploring her work on movement. Over time I developed a more visceral, considered understanding of why I was asking actors to do something. I was filled with a curiosity and desire to find out why this practice worked, prepared to dig deeply and luxuriate in the hours of swings and stretches. I wanted to be in that trusting and rigorous relationship, hungry for the knowledge, the experience and sensations, and over time I shifted from imitation to a more thoughtful approach that led me towards my own teaching style. Balancing one-to-one sessions with the observation of my classes with students, Jane structured the mentorship that shaped my teaching. She witnessed where my strengths and weaknesses lay and observed where my patterns took me and guided me towards becoming a more competent and available teacher of Pure Movement.

And yet this was not always easy. It involved undoing before growth and expansion could follow. Through the mentee/mentor relationship and the depth of exploration it allowed, I was drawn into a process of undoing – I had to let go of habits, both in my teaching and in myself, which had previously supported me. It was a process that made me feel shaken, unsettled. At times I became ungrounded as the familiar revealed itself as less beneficial than I had previously believed.

What follows is an account of the pivotal shifts, in myself and in my teaching, discovered during the mentorship. From my notes, I have elicited the meaningful moments from that time and shared the realisations of my journey. Snippets of conversations with Jane during our sessions are among the reflections quoted in these pages and they give weight to my discoveries – if, at times, they may appear pointed and sharp in tone, it is because they have been removed from the warmth in the room. The reader has to imagine the atmosphere of respect between Jane and me in the working space, where I was eager for her teaching and we built a relationship of mutual trust. Material quoted directly from my notebooks, written during our sessions or shortly after, are also included. Entitled 'Session Notes', they show how I reflected on Jane's words at the time; an echo back to discoveries that at times crept slowly over me and at others hit hard straightaway. These reflections from my mentorship are grouped thematically around Jane's three main categories – content, structure and form. Jane's words are always in italics.

Session notes

———————

Notes Jane gave me: Observation of First Class of the Mentorship.

Need to slow down.

Give each exercise space and time.

Demonstrate much more . . . my job is to show them how to do it.

Use hands on . . . take the time to use my hands.

If I take my time at the beginning, in the first year of their training, I will reap the reward in the second year when the students are able to experience and move.

They (I) need to experience each moment. Don't rush through, don't glide over things

I have a faster rhythm, I need to work with a much slower rhythm

Think about the progression of the class, want to build up throughout the class, start gently, slowly. Trish always started slowly and gently, either on the floor or standing then build up the dynamic from there.

They need to learn to stand in stillness and sustain focus.

———————

Modelling alignment

Jane's initial focus for the mentorship was to build on my content, to pass on the work and develop my repertoire of Pure Movement. By content Jane meant my embodiment and delivery of the movements, not simply the exercises in themselves; the first step towards this involved the organisation and placement of my body. From early on she brought focus to my physical alignment, specifically inviting more openness across my chest and more engagement through my upper spine, to counterbalance a slight drop in my sternum that brought my shoulders forwards. Jane expressed how vital it was to work on myself, that I ought to reflect an open, balanced physicality back to the actors. *'They will copy you, mimic you.'* My responsibility as a teacher was in committing to my own body's full height and breadth, thereby offering a more positive example to the students. Jane often reminded me that this process was like raising my child: as children learn through imitation, parents try to be positive role models. Psychotherapy uses the term 'modelling' for demonstrating ways of being to clients. Jane encouraged me to do the same – to become more conscious of my own alignment and model an open, balanced physicality to the students.

> *Your collapse! You need to keep working on it. You have to incorporate good placement at all times. Good organisation of the body, good placement; this is the starting point for dynamic movement.*

Over the first few months of the mentorship, notes to encourage better placement through my own body appear regularly. Having been reminded about my physical habits in previous trainings, Jane awakened a deeper curiosity. I often reflected on why this was important as a starting point for dynamic movement. Intellectually I knew that alignment was necessary for all acting but I had not yet developed an embodied understanding of it. The possibility of choice is essential and thrilling for actors – to be able to reflect the varied traits in humanity, to find musicality and spontaneity. I sometimes wondered whether such a strong focus on alignment and organisation might quash the actors' playfulness and dampen their ability to make choices. With sustained and gentle focus on lengthening through my spine, however, I noticed that my habitual tensions were slowly easing and, over time, I found more openness across my chest. I felt more ease, more fluidity through my body that allowed me to navigate through the movements without unnecessary effort. *'Maximise, don't minimise'*, Jane would ask me, occupy the maximum space as possible through the body to feel the fullness of the movement. I started to encourage my students to do the same – to resist making small movements and thus limiting their sensorial effect. With a more balanced and strong alignment, they were more capable of maximising without force and of not letting their habits define or limit their experience. This led to greater clarity in their creative choices. For me too, the choice to stay open felt stronger and more alive. Slowly my students began to see what I was offering them as a teacher and realise they could find for themselves the organisation and placement of their own bodies.

Lifting the heart

Come into your back more, really engage the middle of the spine and lift out of pelvis. Lift your heart . . .

Jane spoke frequently about *'lifting the heart'*, a poetic way to encourage an opening of my sternum and chest, to steer me towards better alignment. But it was also practical advice. To find this 'gentle lift', I had to commit to strength and stability through the centre of my body, with a sense of expansion through my spine. The skeletal structure of the spine gave guidance for the muscles to follow. The more I embodied movements that connected to my spine, the more I was able to release around the tail bone and hips, letting my pelvis rest where it needed to rest. This in turn helped my spine to lengthen and my head to balance effortlessly on top. My sternum was then in a balanced place, not collapsed nor pushed forwards, and expression could flow freely with clarity and choice. By learning how to fully inhabit my own body, to discover a connection to my physical instrument that felt empowering and freeing, each movement would also be fully inhabited – lifting my heart was a way to make it possible.

In terms of teaching, it became clear that it was of prime importance how I chose to communicate the embodied nuance of these movements to my students. If I fully opened myself up to the sensation in the movements, as I demonstrated them, my students would be encouraged to do the same. By echoing Jane's poetic phrase and regularly asking my students to 'lift their hearts', I discovered that the simplicity of these words always had an immediate, positive effect on their physicality.

Slowing down

_____

You have a fast energy, need to slow it down a little. You need to get in to the
zone yourself. They need to learn something from every part of their body and
you need to feel it through yours too.

Jane often emphasised my naturally fast tempo and encouraged me to take more time
in my teaching, pointing out that I was often rushing through valuable and sensual
moments. My next realisation was that my instinctive physical drive to work at a fast
pace was dominant in my teaching. A love of diverse, competitive activities in my past,
such as Thai Boxing and ballet, fed into that desire to press forwards and drive the
actors and myself onwards. The drawback to having a fast energy was rushing through
the movements in my teaching.

Work with slowness; the world is very fast paced, it is important to slow down
and feel the movement take hold of the body, to feel it spreading through the
entire body.

With Jane's guidance I was starting to understand the fundamental concept that
teaching movement requires time and space to explore the dramatic possibilities
through the body. It is one area of an actor's training that sits in a fully embodied place,
where they can honestly experience how it feels to be in in tune with their dynamic
body before they connect to voice, language and character. By rushing, I was denying
myself and the actors this opportunity. But if I allowed a strong and centred physicality
that would ground me, I could counterbalance my inherently fast tempo and create
some space, both in my body and in the pacing of the teaching. The whole class would
find greater ease and openness, and consequently feel stronger and more distinct
sensations in the movements. We would have time to maximise the movement through
our bodies. This process also revealed time and space for uncomfortable feelings of
vulnerability in myself; a natural response when challenging habitual patterns. My role
as a teacher was to reflect openness and availability back to the students and model
what I hoped to see in them as actors on the stage. Perhaps this vulnerability was a
necessary added quality to my teaching.

Critique

Jane often asked me to commit more fully to the work and to my practice – my patterns somehow seemed to her suggestive of an unwillingness to commit. Frustration naturally crept in as I was figuring out why my commitment was being questioned and how to undo habits and move forwards. In the early days of the mentorship I expected things to change relatively quickly, with a little focus here and there. I was discovering that to shift embedded physical patterns takes time, persistence and commitment.

My mentorship placed me as the student and Jane offered her professional critique of my work. As our work involved the physical instrument, this critique often focused on how I inhabited my body and used it creatively. I noticed a parallel between my experience during the mentorship and the experience of each student I was teaching. Jane's comments were similar to those I offered my students when I asked them to explore their own physical habits, but words of encouragement and guidance centred around the body can sometimes be perceived as criticism instead of critique. Based on my own faltering responses to Jane's observations, I understood that care and sensitivity was required when offering comments to my students. I needed to build a similar relationship of mutual trust and respect as that of mentee and mentor. As I slowed down and found more strength and grounding through my body, I experienced the many benefits of Jane's critique. I was then able to hear her comments with curiosity and care towards myself.

Hands on

You need to keep adjusting them and yourself.

Jane's critique was always balanced with positive and praising words. I often received comments complimenting my use of 'hands-on work'; she could see the students responded well to my input and she encouraged me to use touch more often, with permission from the student. I was reminded that offering physical adjustments to my students through gentle hands-on contact is an essential element of Trish Arnold's movement practice – a little contact on the back of the neck and sternum to encourage lengthening through the upper spine, a hand on the lower back to encourage the pelvis to drop. Subtle shifts of alignment through touch help the actors to sense themselves, to feel the nuanced sensations of more space and balance. They experience these sensations of change rather than intellectualising them. Over time they recognise how to re-organise the placement of their body.

Leading the group

You have to 'withstand' the students. Lecoq says to 'insist' on it. It is apparent that you are not entirely committing so the students can get to you.

Jane wanted me to take full ownership of my ability and lead the class with more certainty. I faltered at various moments and her observations above addressed this concern. For instance, when I lost the focus of a group I subsequently worked hard to entertain them (a common and not always unhealthy instinct in all teachers). My reasoning was simple – if they liked me they would like the work. Yet it was becoming clear that this was not having the effect I had hoped for; the students' reactions were too easily affecting me and taking me off my centre. My challenge was to sustain the grounding I had gained. Jane invited me to resist my desire to change the dynamic in the room when I felt ruffled. In these unstable moments I would often unconsciously choose to spring into a game, surprising both them and myself by changing the direction of the class. I had to remember Jane's gentle encouragement for me and the actors to go deeper into the sensation of the movements right through our bodies, challenge myself to sustain my alignment and openness and not fall back into habit. I did not need to surprise my 'opponent'; it was not a boxing match. I could stay with these uncertain and uncomfortable moments and breathe, in preparation for the next movement to unfold.

Games, anyone can do them, there is no need for you to do them, playing games is not movement, leave these to others and you do the work that others cannot. By taking them into a game it diffuses the work you've already done. It distracts them.

'Le Jeu', or the game in acting is essential and there are many circumstances where intelligently devised games can help an actor to be responsive, impulsive and find the joy in their craft. There is great skill in teaching actors to play. However, this was not my role as a teacher of Pure Movement. Jane could see my predilection to improvisation and all the skills I had developed in that area. She acknowledged how I had been influenced by teachers whose work made seamless connections between the Pure Movement and the more heightened expressive strands. Trish, Jane and I had taught mask, animal and elemental exploration in other movement classes and these areas more immediately invited physical transformation. Pure Movement explores the foundations of physical transformation and the experiences pave the way for honest expression in all areas. When Trish worked with character masks, for example, she could apply the principles of Pure Movement. The students exploring mask could see how it led them directly into the more transformative physical elements in their training and on into their acting. I began to see that there was a space exclusively for Pure Movement, and within Pure Movement there was vast scope for its own expressivity. My mentorship was a time to investigate the purity within the practice and search for a more focused and specific approach to the teaching of Pure Movement. I could enhance the full connection through every moment and every movement. There could be other opportunities to take the work into improvisation, in a different class. I reflected on the possibility that springing into a game in the middle of a class was also coming from my instinct to avoid the more challenging moments; it dispersed the focus away from me and from staying in the moment. Jane urged me to resist pulling off; to stay in my own body was one way of achieving this, insisting that both I and the actors experience the sensuality of the movement and commit to the moment.

> How to make pure movement into a piece of theatre? They need to see theatre in each movement. Even an arch and round needs to have a dynamic. All movement is full of dynamic.

I was discovering that there could be a wealth of expressivity in every moment in a class. Every movement could be taught and experienced with a relationship to expression that comes from within. This expression did not always need to be connected to an external narrative or imaginative stimulus. Trish used to say, '*you do not need to reach for the apple tree, just connect to the desire to reach into high space*'. By making a connection to the unfolding of each movement, every time, it was possible for me and the actors to resist any single movement becoming merely a mechanical exercise. When I observed Jane demonstrating a movement, I saw a fullness in the experience and a sincerity in her expressive desire. I had also observed this quality when Trish Arnold demonstrated a movement. The connection to expression lay in a strong desire – to reach, to drop and let go, to spring into a gesture. The journey of the movement began with an impulse, a need from deep in the centre of the body that radiated out. It was a discovered moment. By modelling a commitment to each and every physical moment,

I had permission to use the fullness of myself, to use the movements themselves to discover my own creativity flowing out of my body.

As I took on Jane's advice and practised more sustained periods of remaining present, I became conscious of the students' attention staying with me. Their ability to hold focus and follow the flow of the class grew alongside my own. By holding on to this insistence, my students were able to discover their own commitment to each moment and they became increasingly aware of when their attention waned. I was holding the space with more confidence, encouraging actors to work with depth and commitment, and allowing them to explore the fullness of their expressive physical capabilities.

Stillness

Stop fussing and fidgeting. You are deferring your strength and displacing it. The students will copy you. . . . It is your responsibility to stop deferring your strength.

Jane would talk about my energy being scattered and noted that I fidgeted every time I spoke. When I communicated something through words, my body shifted about with tiny little movements, my head wobbling slightly. She suggested that this physicality communicated an apologetic, younger and uncertain demeanour. As a strong and capable woman I was surprised to hear this, as I was unaware my body did not support my words or necessarily reflect my determination.

You need to find ways to stop displacing your strength and to own your length, breadth and strength. They, and you, need to learn to stand in stillness and sustain focus.

Using my awareness of alignment I found more opportunities to stand in stillness. I felt an honesty to it, especially when I spoke. Stillness, although challenging at first, allowed me a moment to lengthen and broaden, to connect to an openness and a sense of strength in my body. It also helped me to slow down, to breathe and feel grounded. I could think more clearly. Out of this stillness came a stronger, physical recognition of each movement I initiated and its subsequent journey through my body, where it began and how it travelled – I was able to listen to the experience with an acute sensitivity. Most surprisingly I felt contained within myself; I experienced a self-assurance and a composure in the moments of stillness, an inner strength that supported my emotional exploration through the movements. This containment allowed me to play physically and imaginatively, eliciting a range of human experiences, all grounded in, and returning to, that initial experience of stillness.

I noticed more time to look up and out into the working room with my attention on the students' explorations. I observed how the absence of stillness before and after an exercise affected them. How their unconscious, habitual movements that were barely noticeable to the untrained eye, muddied the students' expression of the experience. The movements that emerged from a place of genuine stillness, however, arrived with more clarity and a perceived sincerity. Trish Arnold always requested a moment of quiet stillness at the end of a movement to acknowledge the experience through the body and its consequence. I could ask the same of my students and encourage stillness as a creative choice and a starting point for an impulse. They too could take ownership of a more certain and unapologetic quality through their bodies.

I wholeheartedly embraced the joy of stillness in my teaching and it became an integral part of my work, both in the classroom and rehearsal room. I discovered that dynamic stillness is a powerful tool for an actor; in performance it creates a moment of dramatic suspense, alive and buzzing with possibilities, and in the classroom, it offers a connection to this theatricality whilst allowing a chance for clarity of thought and movement.

Session notes

––––––––––

Started in chair, Jane noticed my energy and body goes all over the place when I'm talking and I arch in my lower back, so straight away she got me sitting on my sit bones and finding more drop down through the tail. Jane asks me to:

•   sit on sit bones with hands on lap, roll tail under so rounding into back then arch and take upper body over and release down to floor so hanging off chair

•   uncurl very slowly, feeling the drop in the tail and space and length in lower back. But still really lengthening out of pelvis. Place hands palm up on legs to open into shoulders.

Stay still when talking!!! This very hard

Jane put hands on to lengthen into lower back. Floating head, encouraging breath into back and ribs. Feeling for maximum breadth as well as length.

Talked about the work. Need to understand that this work is different to choreography, it is to help actors find their maximum length and breadth to be able to embody these big texts. As Trish said, this work is 'not a replacement to the exercise bike!'

Need to keep working on myself. Difficult to find the time to do all the exercises but need to keep working on standing and sitting, just continual reminders to shift habits.

Notes to self: Many ways to get to same place. I need:
breadth and width across shoulders, lift heart, wider stance, open chest, top of spine going down which lifts heart and length through middle of back.

Jane talked about lifting the heart, I need to lift my heart more.

Play with the sternum and the heart. Feeling. Remember feeling in the chest/heart.

––––––––––

Structure

—————

Jane's next focus for the mentorship was to look at how to organise the journey of a class. She wanted me to find a structure that allowed my students space for development over the course of each hour-and-a-half class, where they could experience the dramatic unfolding of possibilities in the movement work and connect this to their acting. My role was to offer a framework that gave them an opportunity to connect to the sensual evolution of a sequence of movements through their body – as they would explore a character's journey through a rehearsal process.

> *Trish always started slowly and gently, either on the floor or standing and then built up from here.*

Jane gave me a simple framework; start slowly and build up to more dynamic, bold and demanding movements, always encouraging the movement work to become an expressive and dynamic piece of theatre. Take my students on a journey of discovery throughout each class.

> *Really teach and break things down, don't just skirt over things. Organisation of the body is much harder than you think, it has to be precise, accurate.*

Jane often talked about Trish Arnold's art of breaking down a movement, and, inspired by her own tutelage under Trish, she wanted me to develop this aspect of the teaching. Jane encouraged me to give time to discover the exercises growing, expanding step by step. This would help me to bring light to the creative journey of the whole class. First, I was to allow the necessary space and time to explore the fundamentals: alignment, a relationship with gravity and organisation of the body in space; I needed to play with these using a precision that allowed time for imaginative connections. The next step was to bring together the release of weight, breath and a connection to internal and external space using swings, followed by experiencing the fluidity and three dimensionality of the spine. This led towards undulations and full body swings that speak to the stronger sensation of risk and release. Each class could end with opportunities for the actors to play more freely with each other. Through the journey of a class the actors' focus travelled from an internal awareness to a more external one that included others in the room and out into the space itself. I needed to be clear about where I was taking the students and where I wanted them to arrive at the end of a class. Each class would have a shape, it would be heading somewhere and building into something.

Following Jane's clear structure, and holding on to these principles, gave the students' imagination time to expand as they had a clear process to own. They could experience and recognise their personal development through a class and even be surprised by their physical capabilities and strength of imaginative connections as they journeyed through the progression of movements. Within this structure I could work through each part of the body avoiding injury, every part warmed up, stretched, engaged, and we could then experience *the exploration of the dramatic possibilities of movement.*

Specificity

They, and you, need to experience each moment. Don't rush through and glide over things. If you take your time at the beginning, in the first year of training, you will reap the reward in the second year when they are able to experience more.

Jane's prompts to work with specificity through a structure revealed a space for depth of feeling. It allowed me time to connect imaginatively to a vast spectrum of emotional possibilities. Unsettling feelings were a necessary part of this experience and could be contained within the movements themselves. I thought back to my work on the psychiatric wards, where I was profoundly moved by those struggling with acute mental illness, aware of their unfiltered expression. I began to encourage actors to explore the huge variety of human emotion within the supportive boundaries and safe environment of a class. It was the precision in the Pure Movement that enhanced the possibility of containment – it held my own emotions, a containment that did not exist for me in the psychiatric environment. Teaching with precision and accuracy in each movement offered a deeper connection to the experience and allowed deep-rooted shifts to occur through the body. Jane often reminded me that her physicality only really shifted through Trish Arnold's teaching – her insistence on specificity led to honest expression and created real and lasting change.

Weight

It is about release; the release of the breath, of words, a release of the language from the body. Need to find the honest release.

Jane insisted that I fully and honestly connect to the weight of my own body. I began to explore this sensation of letting go into the natural force of gravity with more depth; the precision in the movements helped me to have a more vivid experience of specific areas of my body releasing. By connecting this release to an exhalation I could experience a physical and emotional surrendering; a yielding, giving up the weight of my body into gravity. A simple spine roll, for example, when taught with an honest and thoughtful connection to weight, became far more detailed and creative than I had ever realised. Starting from standing, there is a forward release of the head. By acknowledging the heaviness of the head there is then opportunity to feel each vertebra through the spine as it rounds over and releases down towards the earth. The weight of the arms connects to gravity as the torso rolls down through the spine. There are then subtle shifts of weight through the feet, hips and legs until there is a sensation of the torso, head and arms hanging freely from the base of the spine. The flow of breath supports the whole journey. These details connected immediately to various imaginative implications – perhaps a heaviness, or inwardness, or a desire to close away or give up as I breathed out into the release, for example, followed by a feeling of unfurling and opening out with possibility as I uncurled upwards through the spine, returning to standing with an easy uprightness and balance.

There is a pervasive cultural understanding in the West that we ought to lift up and away from the earth and pull up through our bodies. My childhood devoted to ballet placed a strong focus on striving for that upwardness, to come away from gravity, not give in to it. In the Pure Movement work, by contrast, the focus is on a balance between gravity and levity, and how these two energies respond to each other. I was discovering that there is a fundamental difference between letting go and collapsing; letting go requires organisation of the body, without affecting the flow of breath. The relationship between specificity and weight spoke to me with such strength, that I found I could insist on the accuracy and simultaneously find a wealth of expression in each moment. At the same time, my awareness of the complex reasons why actors consciously or unconsciously resist this release was growing, and I was recognising that it takes time, patience and repetition to gently insist on an honest release at every opportunity.

The swings

———————

The swings are one of the fundamental aspects of Trish Arnold's movement practice. Here the play between gravity and levity is fully explored. I had been using the swings in my teaching for several years and knew on some level how vital they were to actors in training, but had enjoyed the experience of them without making deeper connections. Jane frequently spoke about the importance of the work Trish had done by modifying the swings originally designed for dancers, and adapting them for actors. The swings required a relationship to release, a rebound motion and free flow, and could be explored through one or many areas of the body, such as one arm or both, a leg or the whole torso. They travel from a point of suspension away from the centre of the body – a gesture out to wide or forwards in the space, for example, and fall into a drop where the fullness of the release is experienced. A rebound motion follows the drop into gravity and reaches a new point of suspension where the direction of the swing reverts back again. The journey continues with natural momentum and free flow, and by repeating each swing several times their effect is multilayered. Fundamentally, the swing releases tension and promotes an ease of motion. A momentary release, or bounce through the knees, at the precise moment of drop connects the upper and lower body. My work with Jane was opening up a new level of understanding – with each swing, I began to experience a relationship between the centre and periphery of my body, to near and far in the physical space, and a sense of effortless continuation. Breath flowed freely, a suspension became a moment of risk, and I felt sensations of joy. By inhabiting every one of these moments, I experienced a sense of being totally present, not knowing what may come next, yet ready and open for this moment to arrive. I identified this as exactly what an actor needs. With each swing I experienced a sharper awareness of how they related to a natural human need for weight, breath and movement.

> *The drop ... this is a big one. If the actor is holding on then everything in acting is dishonest.*

This comment from Jane resonated deeply with me. It allowed me greater awareness of when my students were holding on. I found different ways to play with release so they could become equally conscious of their own resistance to gravity. Trish used to say that the swings were a powerful tool to help the release of breath and impulse; how they connected deeply and organically to the desire to speak as well as gesture became a frequent exploration in my teaching.

Demonstration

Need to demonstrate much more. Let them see the dynamic and impulse through your own body.

Throughout my notes the word 'demonstrate' appears repeatedly. Jane urged me to show students, with my own body, what I expected from them and what I would like them to explore for themselves, rather than relying on vocal instructions. She suggested I follow a simple teaching structure: demonstrate a movement, observe the students exploring the movement, demonstrate again, observe, and then offer adjustments if necessary. If I always committed to balance specificity with embodiment while demonstrating each movement, the students could observe how it connects to the human experience; they would have the possibility of witnessing the strength of physical communication and how movement work relates to their acting. This would be followed by the experience through their own bodies and imaginations – to achieve this, they needed time to observe.

All acting begins with observation, an observation of human life. This is a skill one must learn; there can be no presumption that actors in the beginning of their training know how to observe – how to really see. By demonstrating the movements and insisting they observed me with stillness, space and balance through their own bodies, I could encourage them to commit to a sustained presence and stay in the moment. This helped the students to practise supporting big thoughts through their bodies when acting; they were practising sustained attention every time they observed me, then committing to the fullness of an embodied moment for themselves. By demonstrating, I was also stretching my own ability to stay present, as I could not pull off and disconnect.

I also had to demonstrate with all the sincerity and emotional availability I would like to witness on stage, to let my students know it was OK to experience these qualities. To demonstrate every time was daunting; it was revealing. I had to calm my concerns that what I had to offer might not be enough and that I might lose the actors' attention. In Pure Movement all you have is yourself, no words, no script in hand, no music to dance to, nothing to hide behind. It was just me – the pure expression of my desire. Vulnerability is strong, even if we think it isn't. I had to find an inner strength to demonstrate every movement using the totality of my physical instrument, knowing it may reveal a vulnerability. And over time this became another form of emotional containment as I learnt that strength and vulnerability live side by side. Pure Movement allowed me to explore the wealth of human expression, and by demonstrating, I was giving others permission to do the same.

The more I practised this honest demonstration, this modelling, the more I observed the sharpening of the actors' focus; they observed me without commenting, with openness, empathy and a sense of mutual respect. When it was their turn to explore the movements, I witnessed them challenging themselves to go deeper into the experience. How moving to be in the presence of a room full of people of all ages, from all backgrounds, all exploring their own sensory, imaginative world and sharing all this may reveal. My confidence grew; it was incredibly empowering to know I could commit to being seen. I could insist on rigour and commitment every time I taught, with an understanding of how hard this can be, and with gentle encouragement.

Form

The final category in Jane's mentorship was form, in which content and structure flowed together to create a stronger sense of a whole. My growth already felt immense; now Jane's focus was to gather all I had learnt and foster my own teaching style. Like all students, I had imitated those who had previously taught me, in particular Wendy Allnutt and Danny McGrath, who trained me during my Masters Degree at Guildhall. Both had their own unique approach to teaching Pure Movement. Jane could see that I had not yet found my own voice and was still leaning towards imitation. My own approach required further nurturing. My teaching could then be influenced by those who had left their mark, yet wholly driven by my own creativity and following my own flow. Soon after Jane's emphasis on more frequent and consistent demonstration, the next most repeated note was 'talk less'.

Session notes

————

My resistance is also noticed through my demonstration. Not really taking the time to demonstrate clearly and with confidence.

Need to be prepared to expose yourself. For them to really see you, honestly investing in the work. To see the dynamic and beauty in the movements.

Then they will mimic and try to discover it themselves. Need to demonstrate much more.

They don't have an impulse so no good telling them to move from impulse, means nothing to them. It is an empty instruction. They can discover it through observation then self-discovery. Let them see the dynamic and impulse through your body.

Jane watched end of my class with the E1's. Afterwards we spoke of the dilemma over wanting students to find accuracy in the movement but also wanting them to find engagement with the movement. It is tricky to find the balance – if I work too hard on accuracy, they never have the space to engage with it, to really connect with the expression of the moment. But if no accuracy then it can be unsafe and lacking in precision and detail.

Thought today in class that I cannot adjust everything, need to focus on one area and then let other stuff go otherwise it overwhelms them. All about finding the right balance.

Need to let the musicality come out through the drum, create a real dynamic with it, this will help the students find a dynamic.

Work with the desire. How to encourage actors to find the desire to move, desire to stretch or reach or close in. Has to be an internal pull, feel it from the centre of the body. Again it is about the breath.

————

Embracing silence

—————

Have picked up a habit of 'talking'. Your voice goes on and on, almost shouting out instructions – you don't end up hearing anything and it's a bit like the army or sports training. It loses all its feeling.

Through Jane's candid comments I was made aware of how much I talked through my demonstration of the movements and talked over the students' time for exploration. I was guided towards more silent demonstration and less vocal instruction. Jane wanted me to show the students the movements with silence and let my body do the talking, to give the students time to observe the expression in the movements without my voice affecting the encounter. I was also encouraged to remain vocally silent when it was the students' turn to explore the movements, allowing them to experience the moment through the body, influenced by the beat of the drum without it being cluttered with words.

Can be more dynamic with the drum. Find the light and the dark, shades, rhythm, weight, all through drum. Play and be more creative with it.

I had always used a drum in my teaching, as did Trish Arnold and all those who had taught me. Jane asked me to develop more musicality through my drumming and explore how to use the language of the drum to create dynamic rhythm changes, suspension and flow. The drum would become the guiding voice. Jane pointed out that unnecessary talking disconnected us from our bodies and overshadowed the drum's language. For the students, they worked hard to follow verbal instructions and to interpret them, and for me the words interrupted my own connection to flow. I needed to allow the journey of the class to flow from one movement to the next, where vocal silence could be used as a tool for embodied learning.

Session notes

———————

Talking is just giving instruction; it doesn't allow them to discover the moment or a dynamic. It blocks discovery.

Resistance from me. The incessant talking is resistance from me to wholly commit myself. It is a block between myself and the work. I need to take a RISK, be prepared to be vulnerable.

I am talking way too much! The constant talking separates them from the work.

I have to let them experience the work, to give them the space to discover things. Talking takes this away from them. Denying them the chance to 'experience'.

They were disconnected because you were talking too much.

Rhythm of class was coming through my voice and not the drum. They have to feel it through the body. The body speaks, not the voice. Drum provides a rhythm and creates a dynamic.

———————

The disconcerting realisation that my talking was distracting the students from fully inhabiting the movements was hard to accept. But if I had already discovered the joy of stillness, perhaps I could embrace silence and trust my body to convey what I wanted. I reflected on why I was talking through the movements. Perhaps I was still not trusting that standing there, demonstrating the movements to my students through my body, was enough to offer, that my physical language could be dynamic, express my inner sensations and desires, and speak a language without words.

Impulse

––––––––––

The actors have to learn how to express an internal impulse through their own bodies, no good telling them to 'move from impulse' as it means nothing to them in the beginning. It's an empty instruction. They can discover it through observation, then self-discovery. Show them through body, not voice.

If I asked students to 'let the impulse travel from your centre, out through the body', I had to demonstrate my own embodiment of this concept and not rely on vocal instruction. Let them observe how I communicated a desire physically and how I expressed an internal impulse outwardly through my body, and not clutter this moment with words. I realised that their exploration, in silence, would lead them towards a stronger understanding of embodied expression. It became clear that a connection to impulse needs to be taught as a physical experience, as well as an intellectual and imaginative concept, and they all need to exist and work together in acting. Without unnecessary words cluttering the experience of the movements in the classroom, the body can be an utterly expressive and dynamic tool for communication, and speak deeply to us even before we release a single word. My students could take this awareness directly from my class and into the rehearsal room.

Allow the students to use their imaginations. You don't need to enforce a connection on them. Let them discover it. Students switch off with too much talking, they become disengaged and passive. You have to teach them by example, not force, the same way you teach your son.

The idea of not relying on vocal instruction was terrifying to imagine – without the support of language, how could I make myself clear? It was equally terrifying to put it into practice. My desire to fill the space with words was strong, but with practice, the silence, like stillness, became liberating. The experience in a class became noticeably more alive, more visceral, where my students could luxuriate in the movements without words. They were free to listen to their inner sensations and express these physically. The classroom provided a nurturing framework, a place to experience, value and then harness the full creative discoveries.

Session notes

———

I need to invest more myself and give them and myself more space. The constant talking fills the space up with meaninglessness. What's the point of the work if the actors can't discover a language through their bodies.

I am telling them what to feel and what to experience. And how to experience it. This doesn't work!

Question for Jane:

I don't always see what the students need to work on. It doesn't always jump out at me. If I don't see something clearly then I just work through the body, so am I then just working with what I need? Is this OK? Is this just a generalised idea of where they need to go, not specific to any particular students?

We talked about the work being exhausting, that at this stage in my development it will feel hard work. It is hard work; teaching all day, taking it all into my body and teaching too. I am feeling absolutely shattered after a day's teaching and wasn't sure if this was the way it should be? I am seeing results though, a development through the students. I am beginning to see when they honestly connect to a moment.

I need a balance between my own connection and engagement with my body in the work, and their education. Not just about them. I mustn't allow myself to get bored. Need to keep playing and discovering myself.

———

Trish Arnold

Flow

———

Jane highlighted the moments in a class where I interrupted my flow – my focus faltered and a momentary disconnection occurred. She would describe this as 'settling'; an arrest in concentration where I had ceased to be in the moment. When this 'settling' occurred, the following movements lost their expressive connection and became somewhat mechanical. The energy and creative flow of the class dropped and I would fall into repetitive patterns; the students would then merely imitate me without thought and connection. Like an actor forgetting their lines, panicking and not trusting that the text will come if they can just breathe and remain present, I noticed these moments of disconnection and they unnerved me. I couldn't see in my students where they needed to go next or listen to my own creative flow and so I understandably resorted to habits that felt familiar. How could I observe the students' exploration of the movements in more detail, really notice what they offered, then let this inform the flow and direction of the class?

Insisting on stillness and silence in these moments allowed me greater clarity of thought – I could connect to my own thinking. Consequently when I observed the students I could think in the moment how best to encourage them to deepen their own experiences. I could also tune into my own body and sense where the movements needed to go next. Staying present meant I could risk a momentary beat of the unknown, unsure of what may come next yet trusting that my creative flow would guide me. This was the balance Jane spoke about – a receptiveness that effortlessly shifted between what was necessary for my students' development and listening to where my own sensations were taking me. The movement classes became an alive and theatrical experience, where I was in the moment, demonstrating, observing and responding to the dynamic relationship between me, my students and the physical, expressive language of our bodies.

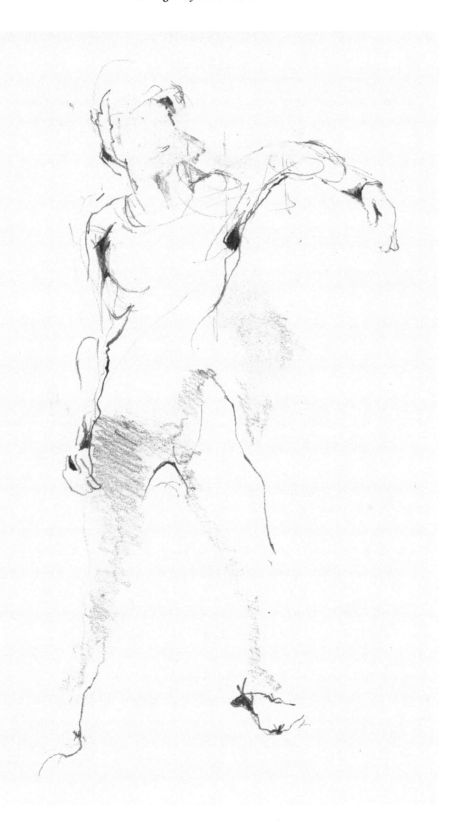

Session notes

———————

What is the difference between a class that works, flows, and one that doesn't?

A class that doesn't work:

It is sticky, jagged, full of stops.

It has the wrong sort of space, the space is filled by my own self criticism, self doubt.

The relationship between me and the actors is off kilter, I am more introverted, more inward looking than out.

I am pushing, pushing for them to have an experience or to have a similar experience to me. Pushing to bring them in to my world.

I am drawn to do more of the movements myself and watch what the actors are doing less, therefore I am not 'seeing', not open to observation and the instinct that leads the direction of the class.

There can often be a strong feeling of dissatisfaction at the end of the class, a sense that something was missing, that something wasn't quite right, didn't quite work or gel.

The actual movements do not flow from one to another, the connections are slightly off. This can sometimes put a strain on the body.

I find myself 'settling', losing focus and concentration. I notice after the moment that I have switched off, I am distracted.

I have lost the balance between technique and expression. When the balance is tipped towards one over the other, the dynamic and the energy of the class is lost. I lose the insistence on expressivity, on a connection to the movements, for them and for me. I allow the actors to settle into a repetitive, disconnected pattern and let myself fall into this pattern too.

I then lose my way in the teaching. It is the sensitive relationship between them and me, the offering and receiving, if one side ceases to offer, there is nothing to respond to.

When a class works:

I see, I notice what the individual actors are doing, who needs adjustment, who needs positive feedback.

There is silence; I demonstrate with fewer words, I resist the desire to speak through their experience, I give them space. This in turn creates a sense of calm, a calm, clear, free energy in the room where an actor can have the space to listen to sensation, feel their way through a movement, a moment. This also creates space for me, space to see, observe, receive what they are offering me. I can notice when an actor is really connecting to a movement or when it is half-hearted, demonstrated and can offer guidance, encouragement.

There is flow, one movement flows into the next. There can be suspensions, changes of direction and dynamic, but the order of the class somehow flows. The use of particular movements to engage different parts of the body seems to make sense, nothing sticks out. They follow with clarity.

I don't run out of time at the end!

There is less effort, less push in my body, the movements have fluidity and ease.

There is a balance between the technical and the expressive.

I am prepared to insist. To work hard to expose my own strength and vulnerability. And to insist on my unwavering focus and attention. This draws the actors in, brings them up to my level.

———————

My own voice

———

As I reached the end of my three-year mentorship, the skills I acquired from Jane Gibson had already transformed my teaching of Pure Movement and deepened an understanding of myself. As I stood in front of a group of students, all hungry for an experience, I was able to ground myself, breathe, allow myself to be available, ready for whatever may arise, and take them and me on a journey of discovery through the movements. By bringing together all the embodied knowledge Jane had taught me – greater alignment and organisation, slowing down, committing fully to each and every moment, demonstrating in silence – I began to find a unique form and flow to my teaching. I was developing my own voice.

Jane used to say:

> *Good teachers are always by your side.*

I could now continue to evolve, to challenge myself every time I was in a classroom and deepen my ability to teach this movement training for actors, knowing Jane was metaphorically by my side.

———

Reflections in the present

———

Any actor learning this craft goes through a process that takes them, slowly, to a place of incredible freedom, of dynamic and honest physical expression that is unique to their artistry. And no matter how you are formed as a human being, or what you bring with you into the work, every individual will make the journey. The more I practised what I received from Jane, the more I noticed my own transformation as a teacher and the freedom and choices that came with it. It was a slow, evolving process with shifts that took their time to embed themselves into my practice.

Through this intimate relationship of mentee and mentor, Jane gave me the gift of clarity in my work. Trish Arnold didn't call it Pure Movement, Jane coined the phrase out of frustration at being asked whether her work was yoga, dance or physical theatre. 'No, it's movement, pure movement.' It is this specificity that speaks to me, the purity in the work. It is uncluttered, skilful, rigorous in the exploration and utterly expressive. Jane opened new pathways and creative possibilities in my teaching, taking me to the next stage on my journey of exploration into Pure Movement. As I faced the challenges this raised, and at times it cost me a great deal emotionally and physically, I recognised it was these challenges that helped me to become more open and available, to grow. And although at times it was undoubtably frustrating and unsettling, I would not change my experience for the world.

Through the passing on of teaching, body to body, I learnt what it really meant to be present, to be 'in my body', willing to risk, to fail, to fall and not to hide. I took ownership of my strengths, embraced my vulnerability and found pride in what I could offer as a creative artist. I learnt to hold a space, to contain and guide actors in training to discover what it honestly felt like to connect with all these aspects within themselves. They too can experience being physically and emotionally alive and be able to express that with clarity and sincerity.

In my teaching today, I regularly witness actors of all ages and all backgrounds going through similar discoveries to those I experienced during my mentorship – not the same as mine, but similar. It is one of the many privileges of working in education. It is always a moving and enlightening experience to be party to the transformation that occurs from the beginning of an actor's movement training, to the end. For each individual goes through their own, often frustratingly slow and at times confusing, journey of discovery. They face similar challenges to my own that come from a process of undoing. And yet each student finds something in themselves they didn't know they had before. Each student develops a new and profound relationship to their body as a means of creative communication. I am conscious of the fragility this type of training awakens in an actor and with compassion and a lived experience, I continually remind them this is part of the journey.

While sustaining the principles Jane gave me, I encourage students to gently question their physicality and to be curious about what they communicate through their body. Through the movement work, they are asked to explore what their physical language offers to the world and to their acting, and to investigate what it feels like to open up new possibilities. It is imperative to accept that our bodies store the experiences we have lived through and that we all naturally develop numerous and diverse physical habits, as well as many unconscious means of resistance, in order to survive these experiences. These may have helped us in the past and will feel safe, but we have a choice to continue using them or to let them go.

I often see new actors in training struggling with the critique that comes with the practice, as I myself struggled, and I try to tread as sensitively as possible into this necessary aspect of the teaching. Before any critique is offered, the students must feel held within a working space where a relationship built on trust and respect has grown between student and teacher, much like that of mentee and mentor. The 'hands on' practice continues today, whenever global pandemics allow for live classes and permission for the touch has been given. During the pandemic, when social distancing rules applied, the absence of touch in my teaching was deeply frustrating and disheartening for both me and my students. It became necessary to use words to describe these nuanced shifts in alignment, and the confusion experienced by the actors was palpable. I am now acutely aware of when a class falters and there is an imbalance between the many components – it is with ease that I am able to gather it back again and follow my flow.

Over the years that followed my mentorship, Jane would occasionally come into a class I was teaching at LAMDA and observe. She would, as always, sit quietly by the side and take notes. We would then meet in a café and discuss her observations. I now mentor other movement practitioners and continue to pass on this work through embodied one-to-one learning. It is Jane's voice that is with me.

As artists, we absorb all that life throws at us, and we need a space where we can translate this experience into something creative and shareable. We can channel it directly into an art form that reflects the vast array of human experiences. The training for this art form is what I offer. Pure Movement moves me deeply, it allows a clear line of unadorned expression that has purity and containment, and it has touched my spirit. It has been a wonderful journey so far.

———————

Three

The Movements

—

*A Collation of an
Embodied Practice*

The movements

———

Those who knew Trish and her work intimately through their body and spirit were softened and opened by her guidance. Each will have their own take on the movements and, as we all do, will have added their own particular essence to the mix. It is my voice that runs through this chapter, one that has come from Trish Arnold, through Jane Gibson, and has been influenced by many more. It is important to note that Trish Arnold's practice was not confined to Pure Movement; it went all the way through to mask and animal work and what may now be considered movement improvisation. Her teaching of Pure Movement supported these areas and took the actor to a place of full expressivity. She redefined and redesigned a movement training for actors that was revolutionary in its time. When I began this project, Trish was very keen for me to clarify that one cannot say she has invented the work but that it has evolved from the many practitioners who have inspired her. The exercises have emerged out of a long career, determined by all those who have influenced her. There are many playful and imaginative movements that I have chosen not to include here; it is a collation of exercises that covers the foundation of Trish Arnold's movement work, one that hopefully reflects the sincerity, specificity and expression of her work, and gives room for one's own development and discovery. My own illustrations of stick people and the simplicity of the explanations are balanced by the beautiful pieces of art by Ben John; they perfectly complement Trish's work – the harmony of technique and expression.

This is not a syllabus; it is an approach to training, a treasury of work that offers precise, accurate explanations of the movements while maintaining the essence of her work – the expressivity of the body. It is an aid, as Trish Arnold herself said:

> *There is so much to be picked up from the teacher that this may also serve to assist in the coaching of the work.*[1]

---

[1] In this chapter, all uncredited quotes in italics are by Trish Arnold.

Key information

Descriptions of the movements are on the left-hand page. On the right-hand page are my own notes, supported by comments I gathered from Trish Arnold and images taken from her notebooks. These notes should act as an aid when exploring the movements physically. To help distinguish them, Trish Arnold's words are in italics.

The movements are in categories and are not suggestive of any order. When exploring the movements insist the body is warmed up and ready to work physically. Start slowly and build on.

'Begin in centre': this is how I describe the starting point for the movements, with feet just off parallel, directly under the hips and arms hanging freely by your side. Legs are long, with soft knees, and you are actively exploring the full length and breadth through your body in stillness. Some movements begin in a wider stance, as noted, with feet turned out slightly more to support the legs. This moment is the beginning of a journey of discovery, full of readiness and possibility. When the movement returns to this stance during repetition, it is not a full stop but a suspension – alert and listening for the next impulse to arrive. When the repeated movements have reached their conclusion, return to stillness, allowing a moment to be curious about their effect on the totality of yourself, others around you and the space you inhabit.

STANCE (cont.)

This image of the stance is to be used in every exercise until it becomes a habit that you carry into all your activity.

If you put your weight in the right place you will feel more powerful, more relaxed, more free.   You will not be able to brace your knees (' the enemy of freedom), and your breathing apparatus will be more available.

Not only this, your balance will be better and you will feel ready to move in any durction without effort.
(It is no accident that all the eastern martial arts lower the centre of gravity)

At first you will probably feel as if you are tipping forward.   This is because many people tip them their torso backwards to compensate for a forward thrust of the pelvis.

Notice that the pelvis is a basin containing your organs. If you thrust it forward they will protrude giving even the slimmest person a "pot-belly". You will also give yourself a back-ache as the weight is thrown onto the lower spine which is not designed to support all that flab!

SO TAKE THE TIME TO PRACTIS THIS STANCE AND REMIND YOURSELF ABOUT IT NOT ONLY DURING THE EXERCISES BUT IN YOUR DAILY LIFE,

Notes written on a typewriter by Trish Arnold. Courtesy author's personal archive.

Key information

Between exercises, hang head downwards, shake out, build up spine, squat and make sure you are relaxed and 'open'.

'The centre of the body': all movement begins with a thought, a breath and an impulse from the centre of the body. The sensation of the movement travels through your body and allows the experience to be discovered. In my teaching, the centre of the body is deep in the belly. When Trish Arnold taught these movements, her language often suggested the impulse came from somewhere else, for example, the ribs in a high rib stretch. This does not neglect the centre of the body, it simply places a little more focus on a specific area of the body.

Every movement requires a free and effortless relationship with breath. Play with breathing through the movements – the suspension, the sigh, a breath into sound, into language, and let it support the movement of your body.

The thing to remember is that every movement has its breath, every thought has its breath. Stop breathing and everything stops. Take it easy, as it comes, don't try to vault six feet until you can clear a foot. If you strain, you get nowhere. What I try to do is unblock energies, let them flow out.

Stretches

All the following stretches allow you to connect from the centre of your body and out into the space, through an impulse or desire to reach. They relate to dimensions in space, specifically high/low, wide/narrow and forwards/ backwards, and encourage an awareness of these dimensions. Always acknowledge the opposing direction through the body as this will ground you and create a dynamic. Stretches enable the ribs to open and expand for breath to flow freely and support your voice. Expression comes from a symbiotic relationship with breath, thought, movement, space and an honest connection to the weight of your body. Try to sense the life and journey of an impulse rather than projecting yourself to an end position – the stretch continues until you feel the conclusion has arrived. Always breathe through each stretch, gently encouraging your body to expand and release rather than forcing it. Play with rhythm, explore differing dynamics and let the movements awaken your imagination.

These rib stretches are fundamental to Trish Arnold's movement training and beautifully represent how her movement work integrated the instruments of body, voice and imagination.

Stretches

STRETCHES

I. Because when they wake up animals always stretch before starting any
other activity we do so too before staring any other exercise.

Don't force the energy, start from where it is with a yawn and let the
yawn "spread" thruogh your arms, spine, neck, rib cage, shoulders, wrists,
ankles and any other limb which may occur to you.

DO NOT TRY TO GET THE IMPULSE THROUGH TO ALL LIMBS IN ONE YAWN.

A stretch is like a yawn in that it always starts with the impulse of the
breath and when that is expended another one starts on another breath.

Make it a new experience every time you do it. Explore new possibilities,
they are endless.   DONT TAKE ANYTHING FOR GRANTED.

Like elastic it is always expanding and then giving in to the next impulse
and the next breath.   IT NEVER,NEVER BECOMES A HELD POSITION.

Repeat mentally and also out loud the words:
BREATH, STR-EH-EH-TCH, GIVE IN.

USE THE SPACE ALL AROUND YOU. Above, behind, below the waist and knees, to
the side, forward. Use the floor.   THINK OF A CAT.

Notes by Trish Arnold. Courtesy author's personal archive.

Yawn and stretch

1   Yawn and stretch from your centre out into the
    space, through every part of your body. Allow
    the desire to stretch take you on a journey, feel
    it come from deep in the centre of your body; a
    need to open out and away. Breathe through
    the stretch.

2   When you have reached your maximum
    stretch, let the weight of the body release;
    it could be just your arms releasing, your head,
    your whole torso, your whole body
    to the floor. Play with the need to let go,
    give up.

3   Once you have let go of the stretch, a new
    desire, new yawn, new breath begins the
    movement again.

Yawn and stretch

Because when they wake up animals always stretch before starting any other activity we do so too before starting any other exercise.

Don't force the energy, start from where it is with a yawn and let the yawn spread through your arms, spine, neck, rib cage, shoulders, wrists, ankles and any other limb that may occur to you. Do not try to get the impulse through to all limbs in one yawn.

A stretch is like a yawn in that it always starts with the impulse of the breath and when that is expended another one starts on another breath.

Make it a new experience every time you do it. Explore new possibilities, as they are endless. Don't take anything for granted.

Like elastic it is always expanding and giving in to the next impulse and the next breath. It never becomes a held position. Repeat mentally and also out loud the words 'Breathe, stretch, give in.'

Use the space all around you. Above, behind, below the waist and knees, to the side, forwards. Use the floor. Think of a cat.

High rib stretch with weight centred

1   Begin in centre, feet slightly wider than
    hip width apart, arms hanging freely by
    side.

2   With an impulse from the centre of your body,
    slowly reach up into high space with your left
    arm, following the most direct route. Weight
    remains centred through feet. Send your gaze
    upwards into high space, keeping space and
    ease in back of neck and shoulders.

3   With an impulse from the centre of your body,
    slowly release the arm back in and down to
    side, taking the most direct route once more.
    Gaze returns forwards.

4   Repeat several times alternating arms.

5   Can develop to both arms reaching into high
    space.

6   Can develop to whole body closing in
    and down, hanging off the spine or a
    loose squat with heels off the floor.
    Repeat a few times and play with pace, breath
    and sound to find dynamic.

High rib stretch with weight centred

Always make sure the journey begins from deep in your centre, and radiates out with breath and desire, letting the centre of your body call your arm back down.

Connect to the sensation of opening out to high and closing in to low, or the sky and the earth, hope and despair. It is about a desire to reach and a desire to give up.

Allow expressive sound to release from the body when playing with a fast dynamic.

It is the honest expression of reaching into space, there does not need to be an imaginative external impulse driving the movement.

You don't need to reach for the apple on the tree, you just reach into high space.

High rib stretch with weight shifting

1   Begin in centre, feet slightly wider than hip width apart, arms hanging freely by side.

2   Let the knees give a little and release the head and shoulders forwards and over so they are hanging.

3   With an impulse from your centre, follow a desire to reach into high space through the right ribs, elbow and hand. Allow your weight to transfer onto the right leg as you reach, lengthening the leg and bringing your head up to see forward in the space. Or look up into high space. Do not rise onto your toes or lift the left hip.

3   Having discovered your maximum reach feeling the space in the ribs, release the breath and drop the arm back to your side, letting the knees bend slightly once more, with the head and shoulders hanging.

4   Repeat several times alternating arms, playing with pace, breath and sound.

With impulse starting from the right side of the rib cage make an unfolding movement vertically, moving through shoulder, elbow, wrist to fingertips until you are stretching the whole of the right side in a vertical line to the ceiling.

High rib stretch with weight shifting

With the impulse of a yawn, stretch the right arm above head . . .

Ribs should expand like a concertina and you should feel as if you are being stretched in two directions; by the arm to the ceiling and by the leg and foot down through the floor . . .

The impulse comes from the ribs and flows through to shoulder, elbow, wrist and to fingers . . .

The end of the movement should look as if you have reached as high as you can. It is a two-way stretch. The right side of the rib cage should be bulging outwards like a concertina . . .

Say re-ea-ch and release, re-ea-ch and release. Never hold the breath, find the breathing for the movement . . .

The movement is done with the quality of a yawn, at the top of the extension you release to centre. Note difference in quality between released and extended . . . get there then give up . . .

Focus on opening the back ribs, keeping the back and chest broad. This will help you to stay balanced without twisting or arching the torso.

It is important to keep the spine long, with the pelvis hanging in its natural position, not tilted forwards or backwards.

Wide or side rib stretch

1 Begin in centre, feet in a wide stance, arms hanging freely by side.

2 With the impulse coming from the centre through the ribcage, elbow, hand and fingers, reach out to the side with the right arm, bending deeply into the right leg at the same time.

3 Having reached the maximum stretch without pushing, release the arm allowing the head and upper torso to hang freely to the right side while keeping the body flat. Simultaneously begin to reach out to the opposite side with the left arm, opening the ribs and transferring the weight on to the left leg as you go.

4 Repeat several times as often as desired, playing with pace, weight, breath and sound.

Wide or side rib stretch

Throughout the movement try to keep the back broad without arching or rounding the spine, with the knees opening out into wide and not collapsing inwardly.

The impulse for the movement as with all the rib stretches is from the centre of the body, into the ribs and out into the space, using breath and an honest desire to reach.

. . . Continue from side to side rather like a wave . . .

As with all the rib stretches, allow your desire to reach continue beyond the periphery of your body out into space.

When you've reached it, don't hold onto the extension. Let it go and continue with a new impulse.

Forward rib stretch

1 Begin in centre, feet in a wide stance, arms
   hanging freely by side.

2 With the impulse coming from the centre
   of the body with a breath, draw the left hand
   over the back ribs and reach into forward space,
   tucking the tail bone underneath you, rounding
   the spine and shifting weight on to the left leg
   as you do so. Either look into forward space or
   a little down towards the ground, keeping neck
   and shoulders soft.

3 Having reached the maximum stretch, feeling
   the back ribs expanding, release
   the arm allowing the head and upper
   torso to hang in forward space and the weight
   to return to centre with knees a
   little bent.

4 Repeat with the right hand drawing over the
   back right ribs and on into forward space,
   shifting the weight onto the right bent leg.

5 Repeat several times as often as desired, playing
   with pace, weight, breath and
   sound.

Forward rib stretch

It is a bit like over-arm stroke in swimming.

When reaching forwards, stroke the back ribs of the same side with the back of your hand to encourage opening of this area.

You will be able to reach much further if you really bend into the supporting leg.

As well as a desire to reach forwards in the space, there is an opposite pull into backward space, this encourages the body to stay balanced and not tip too far forwards.

Weight does not transfer forwards, weight is kept central.

The focus is on opening and stimulating the back ribs. Try not to lock the arm, shoulder or neck. As in all the rib stretches try to continue the flow of the movement.

Think of leaning over or on an imaginary balloon. This will help you retain the position. Embracing or reaching over a balloon.

Arching and rounding the spine 'bird and bear'

1   Begin in centre, feet in a wide stance, arms
    hanging freely by side.

2   Release the knees and bring both arms
    forwards and round to shoulder height
    as if hugging a huge ball, rounding the
    spine as you do so, bringing the tail
    under and allowing the head to follow
    the spine.

3   With the impulse coming from the centre of
    the body, allow the spine to open out into an
    arched position with head and tail moving
    together, arms following the journey of the
    spine and opening out wide into the space.
    Keep the arms at shoulder height throughout,
    letting the palms of the hands open up to the
    space above, with soft elbows.

4   Release the knees and let the body close away
    into a rounded position once more, arms
    following the journey of the spine, staying at
    shoulder height throughout.

5   Repeat several times, allowing the breath
    to flow freely through the body as you move.

Arching and rounding the spine 'bird and bear'

Progression:

1 Drop the weight of the arms during the journey of the spine from bear to bird and back again, allowing the arms to swing from one position to another.

Experiment with released easy breathing, this will help you discover the feeling of fluidity and ease.

Enjoy the sensations of the body closing away and opening out.

Insist on engaging breath to support the movement of the body throughout each journey and the knees release to support the spine.

In position 2 the arms are like the forelegs of a standing bear embracing a large sphere or globe.

In position 3 the arms are like a bird's wings as if it flaps them on the ground or as they do when they seem to be exercising them.

During this sequence of movements find how you can initiate the movement from the knees and the base of the spine. Also find a quality of fluidity, gently rocking not jerking.

Rib stretch

1   Begin in centre with wide stance.

2   With an impulse from the centre of your body, let the left arm lengthen away from the body and spring it up into high space passing through wide.

3   Shift the weight onto the right leg, leaving the left leg long as the left arm reaches over your head out onto the diagonal encouraging the torso to stay flat without twisting.

4   Reverse the journey, taking the arm back up to high space and passing through wide to return to your side, letting the weight shift back to centre.

5   Alternatively you can bend into an opposite stretch with the left knee bending as you reach out on the right diagonal.

Rib stretch with head release

1 Begin in centre with wide stance.

2 Repeat the previous rib stretch, taking the left arm out wide and above your head into high space. Shift the weight onto the left leg in an oppositional bend; the knee of the left leg opening out wide to the left and the gesture reaching out wide to the right. Try not to twist or arch into the spine but sustain full length and breadth through the torso.

3 Instead of returning the arm back the way you came, let it continue its journey, dropping down into its natural position by your side. At the same time, drop the weight of the head and sternum into forward space, bringing the weight through the legs back to centre.

4 Uncurl through the spine to standing.

5 Repeat with the other arm.

   Any drop of the body into gravity must be accompanied by a release of breath, one cannot exist without the other.

   Play with the breath springing into the body with ease as you uncurl, as though about to speak.

Stretches

Stretches ---Cont.

Stance no.3
5. Now Swing the right arm over the head as if trying to sweep the ceiling
withyour fi nger tips
Take your weight onto your left leg and bend the knee , bend the waist
sideways as you reach over your head and reaching over your head to the
side as far as you can.
Relaxand drop the arm coming to a central stance, relaxing both knees.
Sweep left arm over your head and bending the right leg reach to the right side.

6.   Bend both knees as if riding. But with knees pointed over toes.
Arch back, sticking your tail out at the back.
Sweep arms in a wide arc as if wiping a window infront of you and then
feeel as if they are being pulled behind you to meet behind you back.
Your chest will be sticking out, so will your tail, your face to the ceiling
in a distorted sort of position. Rather like a duck.
Then collapse into the head down position hanging arms, head and shoulders
from your spine as in the bouncing.   ALTERNATIVE - SQUAT
Knees are bent throughout this.   THEN PIKE   PIKE

Slowly "build up" through the spine as described in "Dropping down and building
up" till you are standing upright,

NOTE, When you have dropped down bring feet to Stance no. I. before
"building up".

Repeat fromNo. 2 to No. 6.

Notes by Trish Arnold. Courtesy author's personal archive.

The spine

This next collection of movements connect deeply with the spine. As Trish Arnold once said, *'we all forget the spine'*. These exercises increase your awareness of your skeletal structure. They encourage you to find more fluidity and flexibility, which in turn enables length, space and an ability to organise your body with clarity and specificity.

The spine roll down

The spine sustains the entire body. We need to be aware of each section of the spine and its relationship to the whole.

Close eyes. Put the attention on the spine. Think of each vertebra resting one on top of each other in a long jointed column. Starting from the top vertebra let the head slowly drop forwards leaving arms and shoulders loose. Allow the weight of the head to pull the spine downward vertebra by vertebra until hanging head downwards from the hips. Do not keep the knees straight. Allow them to relax as and when necessary as you drop through the spine.

Uncurl slowly building each vertebra up on top of the one below, starting from the base of the spine. Think of them as small building blocks. Carry on until standing upright leaving the head last. Allow the head to rest lightly on top of the spinal column. Think of the column continuing up beyond the top of the head. Leave arms and shoulders relaxed and passive throughout the exercise.

Repeat with a partner pressing on each vertebra in turn to increase the awareness of the process. Partner should check if the shoulders and arms are hanging loosely. Also make sure the head is left until last.

When making any physical contact with a partner, always ask for permission first.

When pressing on a partner's vertebra, the contact needs to be clear but not too firm. You are offering an external impulse to your partner that has clarity of intention, one that they can experience and respond to.

The spine roll down

Try to keep an upwards energy through the back of the legs as you hang from the pelvis, from heels to hips, keeping the knees soft, without stretching too much into the hamstrings. There is an opposite, downwards energy from the tail out through the top of the head.

Keep the legs long as you uncurl through the spine; do not bend into the knees to come up but lengthen the legs as soon as you begin the journey of uncurling.

Play with the breath throughout, the release of breath as you give up and let go, the inhalation bringing you back up into the space.

Pelvic rocks

1 Begin in centre with feet under your hips, feet just off parallel.

2 Release the knees as you scoop the tail underneath you, rounding into the lower back but keeping the rest of the spine long and balanced.

3 With responsive, springy knees, let the tail come out behind you, tipping the pelvis forwards so the lower spine is arched.

4 Repeat this journey slowly several times allowing the pelvis to release into the journey and the knees to be responsive, supporting the movement.

5 Pick up the pace until the pelvis is rocking or swinging from round to arch and back to round, keeping the rest of the spine still and balanced, with breath flowing freely.

Progressions:

Swing pelvis in circle with loose knees. Image: Stir the mayonnaise or porridge to taste!

Combine swinging under and out with circling. Make it into a dance. Click fingers or keep arms above head.

Pelvic rocks

The pelvis should swing or rock like a boat or a swing . . . The lower back and waist are engaged; the upper back and shoulders stay passive.

Image: A wasp is detached at the waist and moves below the waist only.

To help keep upper body still, place hands on head.

Progress to swinging under and out on each bounce. Making a dance movement with hips and pelvis, under and out, with released knees and bouncing movement.

Knees very active and soft and always lead movement of spine. Spinal arching and rounding not safe without support of knees and thighs.

Insist that the knees remain released when the pelvis is tucked under and that the upper body is balanced and not leaning back in the space. This opens the space at the front of the hips.

Insist that the buttock and stomach muscles remain soft and not tense as you rock the pelvis.

Bounces

1   Begin in centre with feet under your hips and just off parallel.

2   Bounce the knees, dropping the weight down through the knees and rebounding back up to full length, several times. Try to keep the head balanced, the spine long and the arms and jaw free.

3   With each bounce progress to allowing the head and torso to drop forwards and over all the way down through the spine until you are hanging out of the pelvis. Continue to bounce the knees loosely leaving the arms and head hanging freely.

4   With each bounce come up through the spine until you are standing once more.

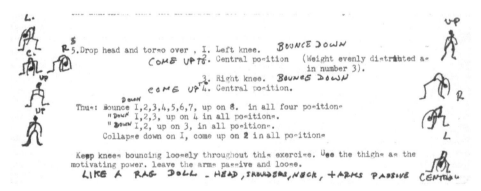

Notes by Trish Arnold. Courtesy author's personal archive.

Bounces

When coming up you should use the thighs not the waist as the impulse (naturally the waist will be used but the motivation for the movement should come from the thighs).

Look for a dynamic of dropping and rebounding in the bounce, it is not a bend and straightening of the legs, but a release of weight down and a spring away from gravity.

The pace or rhythm of the bounces needs to allow time for a drop and a rebound motion, not too quick, not too slow.

Like a rag doll; head, shoulders, neck and arms are passive.

Mark out the spacing in between the 8 or 4 bounces down so the gaps are all equal, try to hit each marker every time. This requires organisation of the body.

Keep the weight forwards and over as you bounce, trying not to let the weight sink back into the heels or send the pelvis into backward space. This requires balance.

Bounces

Sequences:

1   8 or 4 bounces down

    8 or 4 bounces hanging off spine

    8 or 4 bounces coming to upright position.

2   8 down, 8 back up

    4 down, 4 up

    2 down, 2 up

    1 down, 1 up – this is a full drop of the torso
    and a rebound back to full height.

3   7 bounces down and up on 8th

    3 bounces down and up on 4th

    both arms can spring up into high space on the
    last bounce, with or without a rise onto balls of
    feet.

4   Bounce down for 8 with torso turning onto the
    right diagonal and weight shifting slightly on to
    right leg, head and torso dropping over the
    right knee

    8 bounces hanging off spine

    8 bounces back up.

    Repeat in centre, 8 down, 8 hanging, 8 back up.

    Repeat on left side.

    Progress to 4 right, 4 centre, 4 left, 4 centre.

Bounces

The last 2 options require really loose and flexible knees and may not be suitable for beginners.

This is an exercise which introduces the student to the awareness that the motivation for a movement is not always the obvious one.

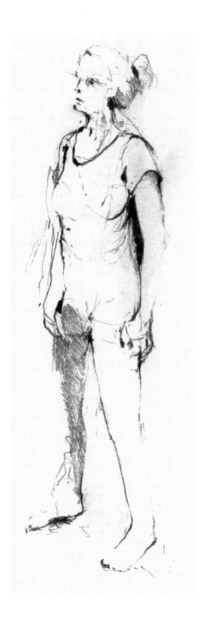

Bounces to sides with torso drop

1 Stand centred with feet slightly wider than hips and slightly off parallel.

2 8 bounces through the knees over to the right side, bending from the hips but with the torso remaining flat to forward space.

3 After the 8th bounce to the side, let the torso drop so hanging off the spine with weight in centre.

4 8 bounces at the bottom with head and arms hanging freely.

5 8 bounces back up to standing.

6 Repeat to the left.

7 Progress to 4 bounces.

Bounces to sides with torso drop

Try not to anticipate the drop by letting the torso twist or the opposite shoulder drop into forward space.

Enjoy the full release only at the end of the 8th bounce to the side.

Try to space the bounces to the side equally, organising the body.

Let a sound tumble out of the body as you drop, it is a big release.

For beginners, the torso can drop to the chest instead of all the way down, build the movement.

Arching and rounding on hands and knees

1   Begin on hands and knees, hands directly under your shoulders and knees directly placed under your hips, your spine long and flat with the head following line of spine and not dropped down.

2   Send the middle of the spine up to the ceiling, allowing head and tail to release downwards so the back is rounded, head hanging.

3   Release the middle of the spine down towards the floor as the head and tail lengthen away from each other and up to the ceiling so the back is now arched.

4   Repeat as many times as desired.

Arching and rounding of spine is fundamental movement exercise. It is used to encourage mobility of spine; by repetitive use of movement the muscles supporting spine are able to strengthen and release.

Arching and rounding on hands and knees

Make sure weight is evenly displaced through the hands and feet and continues throughout, keeping stomach muscles soft especially when the spine is rounding, resisting tightening and shutting off the breath.

Encourage the spine to move as one; the head and tail travel together, the spine rounds and arches in one movement rather than a rippling through the vertebrae.

On hands and knees on floor. Arch spine like a cat. Then push spine towards ceiling to the reverse position called 'round.'

Repeat as often as required. Do this very slowly trying not to engage the stomach muscles. This will seem impossible at first in the 'round' position. Try to breathe into the belly in both positions and keep head as free as possible.

Play with the pace of the movements and add in sound.

Try to keep spine long throughout, avoiding crushing the upper vertebrae in the arch. Try not to sink into it but lengthen forwards and upwards, lifting the sternum and widening the space in-between the shoulder blades.

Arching and rounding on hands and knees

On hands and knees chew into the spine, as if you are trying to connect with each vertebra in the spine. Let the chewing motion be slow and sensual and breathe through the movement. Keep the arms long and weight centred.

Try to make the movement starting at the base of the spine and rippling through to the neck. Do this in both directions. Think of each vertebra separately as in the lowering of the spine in the 'pelvic thrust' but this time the movement starts at the base of the spine.

Don't hurry; try to experience the movement right through the whole spine.

In 'arch' position extend right leg backwards in the air as high as possible without straining. Bring knee in towards head and replace on floor. Repeat with left leg. Check breathing while leg is lifted.

In 'arch' position extend right leg backwards in the air as high as possible without straining whilst keeping the knee bent. Open the knee out from the hip and look towards your knee. Return the knee so the hips are parallel with the floor and bring the leg under the torso as you round into the spine. Repeat a few times then change leg.

Animal drinking

1 Begin in 'folded leaf' position: the pelvis resting on heels, head released onto the floor and arms resting on the floor above your head, a little wider than your shoulders.

2 Come up onto hands and knees with a rounded spine and arms long.

3 Reverse the movement of the spine into an arch with head and tail lifted either as one movement or rippling through the spine from the tail.

4 Keeping tail in the air, lower the chest slowly to the floor, like a lion drinking at a watering hole. Keep the spine arching.

5 Lift the chest back up so the arms are long once more with spine remaining arched on an in breath, surprised, sudden.

6 Reverse the movement of the spine back into a rounded position either as one movement or rippling through the spine from the tail.

7 Drop the pelvis back towards your heels and rest the head. Repeat a few times.

Pluto under the fence or cobra

1   Begin in 'folded leaf', arms resting on
    floor above head, hands wider than shoulders.

2   Lift head off floor and look forwards in the
    space, slide forwards with your chest as low to
    the floor as possible.

3   When you have come out as far as you can go,
    use the momentum created in the slide to lift
    upper body off floor so your arms are long,
    head is balanced on top of spine and
    lengthening away from tail. Lower body
    remains released into the floor.

4   Let the tail draw you back in again to folded
    leaf OR tuck the toes under and lift the lower
    body off the floor about an inch into *Lifted
    Cobra*. Spring tail up into high space with arms
    and legs long, stretch into hamstrings with a
    gentle treadle through the feet.

Upper spine exercise

1 *Stand long. Point finger at chest. Shrink away from it until chest is concave and depressed looking.*

2 *Now imagine finger pointing between shoulder blades. Shrink away from it by pressing spine forwards as if it is going through chest.*

3 *Come back to normal stance.*

4 *Now repeat without actually pointing finger, coming into normal stance between each arched position, i.e. normal, concave, normal, arched, normal, etc.*

During this exercise avoid arching or rounding the small of the back. Keep it isolated from the upper back.

Connect the breath to the movement of the sternum and let the knees remain soft throughout.

Try to resist the shoulders becoming too involved, keep them soft and let them follow the journey of the sternum.

Let the head follow the movement of the spine and not drop forwards or tip too far back.

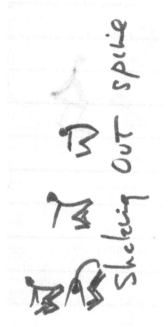

Spine shake outs

1   Begin in centre, let the head release and roll down through the spine until the upper body is hanging freely.

2   Round up through the spine halfway with the head and arms still hanging.

3   From the tail, ripple through vertebra by vertebra into an arched spine with head lifted and looking forwards then immediately begin to release back down to hanging, letting go of the weight of the head once more.

4   Repeat this motion, rounding up and arching down in a sustained rhythm without any dropping of weight.

5   Once this is understood through the spine, add in the drop and rebound; let the whole torso drop into gravity as you arch down and rebound away from gravity as you start to round up through the spine to halfway.

6   Continue this movement with a quality of shaking out the spine, rippling through the vertebrae with ease and breath. Rest after 8 ripples.

7   Uncurl slowly through the spine to full height, noticing the energy and length through the spine.

Spine shake outs

This movement is a natural undulation through the spine, the same motion that occurs effortlessly when we walk. It is important to find the release in the movement, the dropping and rebounding of weight. It is this that allows the movement to have a natural freeing quality to it. If there is too much hold through the neck and shoulders, then the body is engaging muscle and will cause strain.

The head and arms follow the ripple through the spine and respond naturally without tension, try not to place the arms.

Use the image of a string of pearls or shaking out a silk scarf, to give the movement a sense of ease and space, a natural releasing through the vertebrae as you shake out.

This movement requires free flowing breath to support the body in its natural flow. Allow sound to tumble out of the body.

You can progress to shaking out the spine on diagonals, 4 left, 4 centred, 4 right.

It is important to take your time learning this movement.

Sea serpent

1   Begin with feet a little wider than hip distance apart.

2   Spring both arms up to high space with palms facing forwards then drop hands from wrists so fingers pointing forwards in space.

3   Round down through spine with hands leading movement as if diving into the sea until torso and arms hanging freely, palms of hands now parallel with the floor, fingers still pointing forwards in space.

4   Sway torso from hips and allow fingers to softly search around the legs and feet, loosening and breathing.

5   Let the hands lead the movement back up to standing, arching through the spine to end with arms reaching up into high space once more.

6   As the hands release from the wrists, let the tail drop and spine returns to long and broad with no residual arch.

Begin with using one arm at a time, hands and fingers forwards and 'see'.

Curl over with whole body, keeping elbows bent, and sink into the sea, swim or not with hands and torso.

Bring your palms out in front, fingers up, arch through spine out of the sea and see at the top, can do in continuous motion without swimming.

Repeat with other arm, then with both arms.

Standing undulations

1   Begin with feet in parallel and hip width apart.

2   Bend into the knees and begin to shift the thighs into forward space.

3   This movement ripples up through the body as the pelvis shifts into forward space creating an arch through the lower spine.

4   As the undulation continues up through the body, the sternum opens creating an arch through the whole spine.

5   The head follows lastly returning to a point of balance on top of the spine. As the whole torso finds balance the spine comes into its full length and breadth.

6   Progress to allowing the whole torso to arch forwards and down until you are hanging out of the pelvis.

7   Repeat the undulation from this point, with the knees releasing, the thighs, the pelvis, the sternum coming up and into forward space as you return to full height.

Allow this to be one continuous flowing movement; it is an undulation travelling upwards through the spine, then take your time arching back down through the spine. This is a big movement, engage the breath and keep a sense of space through the spine.

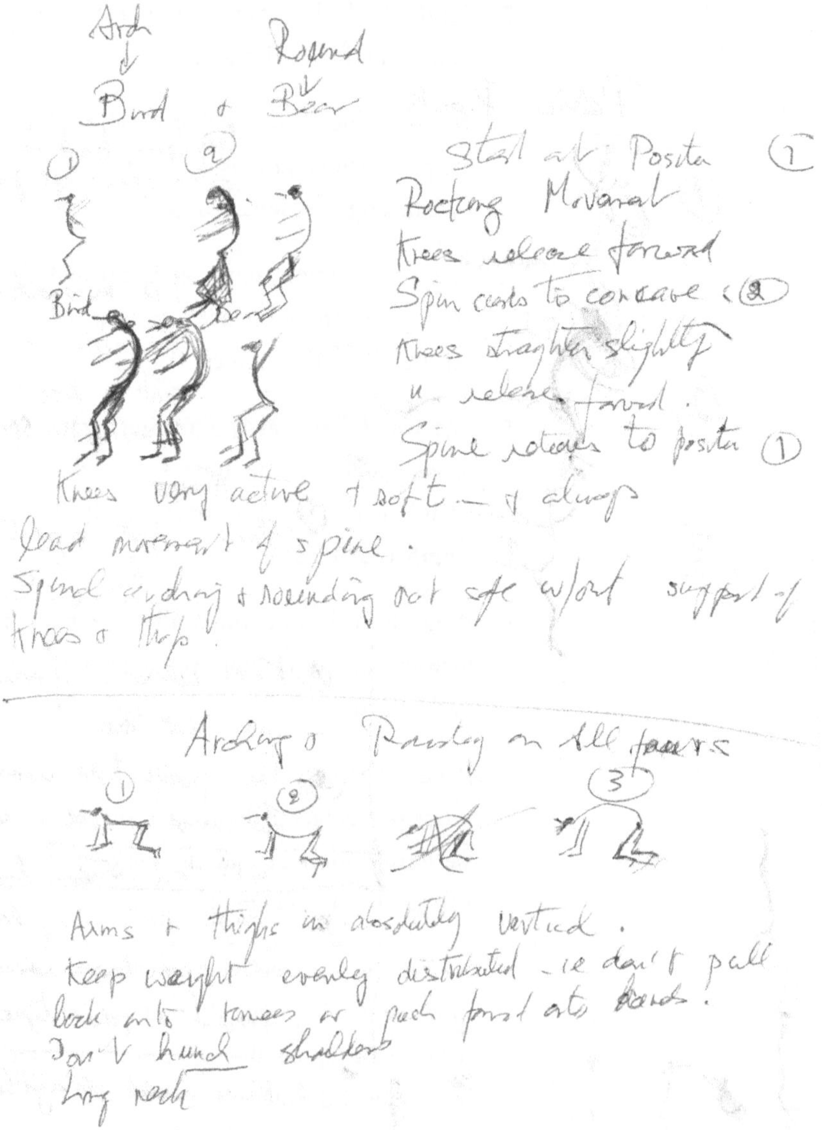

Arch ↓ Bird & Round ↓ Bear

(1) (2)

Bird

Start at Position (1)
Rocking Movement
Knees release forward
Spine curls to concave (2)
Knees straighten slightly
& release forward.
Spine releases to position (1)

Knees very active & soft – & always
lead movement of spine.
Spinal arching & rounding not safe w/out support of
knees & hips.

Arching & Rounding on All fours

(1) (2) (3)

Arms & thighs in absolutely vertical.
Keep weight evenly distributed – ie don't pull
back onto knees or push forward onto hands!
Don't hunch shoulders
Long neck

Notes by Trish Arnold. Courtesy author's personal archive.

Floor work

Trish Arnold often began or ended a class on the floor. By letting go into the earth, you can discover an honest relationship to the weight of your body. There is greater opportunity to slow down, breathe deeply, and explore areas of the body through gentle movement, with an effortless specificity. Through the dynamics of stretch and release, open and close, these movements all create a sense of space within your body and an ease and fluidity in motion.

Floor exercises are to be used whenever you feel stiff and tired.

Pelvic rocks on floor

1 Lie on floor in semi-supine position with feet close to buttocks, knees to ceiling and arms out to sides on floor.

2 Gently roll the pelvis away from the centre of the body increasing the natural arch in the spine. Let the pelvis drop back to into the floor with a release of breath. Repeat this a few times.

4 Then roll the pelvis towards the centre rounding into the lower spine a little but keeping the weight of the pelvis on the floor. Repeat a few times.

5 Alternate the movement of the pelvis between arch and round, starting with a release in between each journey, then progressing to a loose, wobbly rock between the 2 points.

6 Roll the pelvis from side to side, focusing on dropping the weight of one hip into the floor, rather than lifting the other.

7 Roll the pelvis around in a circular motion, enjoying the weight and the flow of the movement.

Pelvic rocks on floor

Connect to the weight of the pelvis and imagine you are moving the skeleton rather than needing to use muscle.

Do not lift the pelvis off the floor when rolling under and rounding into the spine, this is a tiny movement and requires a rolling motion without engaging the hip flexors or the stomach muscles.

Engage the breath through every movement to help the flow and ease of motion and consequently the release of tension around the hips and pelvis.

Pelvic rocks on floor advanced

1 Lie on floor in semi-supine and bring both knees up onto the torso, letting the weight of the legs go so the hips and pelvis are open.

2 Rock the pelvis forwards and back in a loose, gentle motion, allowing the head to respond to the movement.

3 Rock the pelvis side to side staying in-between the protruding bones at the back of the pelvis.

4 Circle the pelvis one way then the other, in small, gentle circles, as if massaging the lower spine and sacrum.

5 Hug your knees into your chest to rest.

6 Repeat once more.

7 Place a hand on each knee and draw big slow circles with your knees, oiling into the hip joints, both knees opening out together and coming in together.

8 Keep the knees together, letting the arms fall onto the floor at shoulder height, roll the pelvis to one side and drop the weight of the legs to the floor, head turns in opposite direction to the knees. Breathe into the stretch.

9 Repeat on the other side.

Pelvic rocks on floor advanced

This movement requires open, flexible hips and can cause some strain if carried out by inexperienced actors.

Allow the head to rest on the floor and keep the neck really free so the head responds to the movement of the pelvis.

Add in gentle sounds to the rocking motion as you progress.

If the hips or inner thighs begin to feel tense, bring the knees in a little or rest whenever you need.

Pelvic thrusts

Lie on back in semi-supine position with heels as close as possible to the buttocks, slightly further apart than the hips. Knees to ceiling.

Breathe in and as the breath leaves the body thrust the pelvis towards the ceiling as high as possible. Put hands on buttocks and push a little higher so that there is maximum arch of the spine.

Place hands on floor. The weight is now being carried on the feet and shoulders and the thighs are strongly engaged in supporting the weight of the pelvis. Check the breathing.

Keeping breath easy start to lower spine to the floor vertebra by vertebra starting at the point nearest to the neck and finishing as near the coccyx as possible. Do not worry if this cannot be carried out literally. It is an image to help the spine to be active. The spine should feel very long when it has returned to the floor. Think of it reaching to the heels. Release all joints and breath.

Adjust feet if necessary and repeat 3 more times. Feet; although not parallel they should not be very turned out, as this will prevent the correct engagement of the thighs.

Pelvic thrust variation; Place arms beyond head on the floor. Leave them there while the spine is returning to the floor. This gives a big extension to the rib cage. Always release after the action and keep breath going steadily throughout the movement of the spine.

Floor work for shoulders two arms

1 Lie on floor in semi-supine position, arms resting on floor out wide at shoulder height.

2 Slowly raise both arms off the floor and up towards high space, reaching out and away from your centre as you go.

3 Find a point of balance with the shoulder blades resting on the floor and both arms balancing vertically at shoulder width with palms facing each other.

4 Reach upwards with both arms, opening through the back of the shoulder blades, then let the weight of the shoulders drop back into the floor, keeping the arms suspended.

5 Repeat a few times.

6 Let both arms return out wide to the floor at shoulder height on a slow count of 20.

Floor work for shoulders two arms

Encourage the neck and jaw to be free of tension and the head respond to the lift and drop of the shoulders.

Progress to spiralling the arms inwards or outwards on the lift and releasing the spiral as the shoulders drop back into the floor.

Connect to breath, space and weight.

Progression:

1   Take both arms off the floor and up into high space. Turn palms of hands towards the feet.

2   On a slow count of 20 return both arms to the floor above your head.

3   Stretch the arms on the floor away from the hips and release, repeat a few times.

4   Stretch the arms away from the hips bringing them back into wide at shoulder height during the stretch, releasing the weight when you get there.

Floor work for shoulders one arm

1 Lie on the floor with legs up onto the chest and knees together, arms out wide at shoulder height. Let the weight of the legs drop to the left and the head fall in the opposite direction.

2 Lengthen the right arm away from your centre then slowly lift the arm up into high space, following the journey of the hand with your gaze. Let the right shoulder rest on the floor with the arm balancing vertically.

3 Reach upwards with the right arm, opening into the back of the shoulder and letting the head respond freely to the movement, then drop the weight of the shoulder back into the floor, leaving the arm suspended. Repeat as often as desired.

4 On a slow count of 20 return the right arm to the floor at shoulder height, following it with your gaze.

5 Sweep the right arm over your head to rest on top of the left so you are lying on your left side. Reach out with the right arm once again opening through the back of the shoulder blade, then let the whole of the arm spring across the chest and open back out into wide. Repeat as often as desired and then with the other arm.

Add in the use of sound or text. Keep the neck and jaw free from tension.

Stretches on floor crescent moon

1 Yawn and stretch on the floor like a cat waking up, stretching away from your centre and releasing at the end of the stretch, letting the breath flow freely throughout.

2 Close the body in and roll onto your side in a foetal position.

3 Open out from the centre of the body into an arch with hands and feet stretching away from each other, remaining on your side, and into a crescent moon position.

5 Feel the body closing back in to foetal. This can occur slowly or spring back in suddenly with the breath.

6 Repeat on the other side.

7 Lie on the floor on your back, stretch from the centre of the body out through the diagonals of your body, one hand and opposite foot lengthening away from each other with breath supporting the stretch, releasing at the end of each stretch.

8 Stretch away from the centre through all four peripheral points and release with an exhalation.

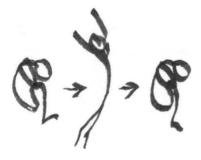

Floor work

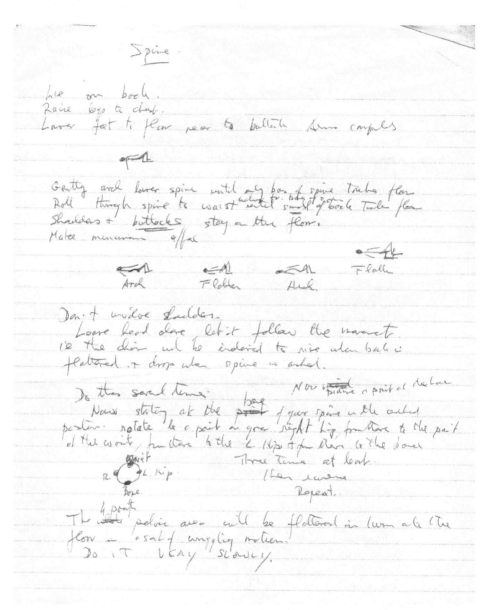

Notes by Trish Arnold. Courtesy author's personal archive.

Arm and body swings

Trish Arnold's swings connect with impulse and release, work deeply with the natural breath, and promote an ease and pleasure of movement. There is a relationship between gravity and levity in each swing – a release of weight into gravity, followed by a rebound into levity which flows into a moment of suspension before the release begins again. The swings travel through space, connecting the centre of the body to the periphery and beyond. Each swing described in this section can fill you with a sense of freedom, an expressive and unspoken language that connects deeply to your desire to gesture, speak and communicate. Some are beautifully simple, others demand more totality and precision in organising the body. And all connect to the dramatic potential of risk.

Connect the weight of a swing to free-flowing breath.

Notice an opposite energy that travels in from the limbs to the torso to avoid strain and over extension.

The knees release organically to support and enhance both the drop and the rebound of the swing, but their gentle bounce is a response to the impulse rather than a controlled movement or plié.

There are many variations of the swing, those noted here are the foundation of Trish Arnold's swings. Play with sequences, with directions in space, and always commit to a specificity, an impulse, the breath, and the drop and rebound.

One arm swing into wide

1 Begin in centre with feet wider than hips, arms
   hanging freely by your side.

2 With the spring of an in-breath, let the left
   arm lengthen away from the centre and out
   into wide space, suspending at shoulder
   height.

3 Release the arm, letting it swing into
   a closed position across your chest, suspending
   for a moment as it changes direction before
   letting it swing back
   into open and wide position, where you
   started.

4 Repeat as often as desired, letting the knees
   release with the drop of the arm and the body
   remaining stable.

5 Progress to letting the arm swing over the top
   in full circles.

6 Repeat the swing with the other arm.

One arm swing into wide

Play with the drop and suspension of the swing, and the joy in the continuation of the free-flowing movement.

Let the breath support the swing, adding in sounds or words as the swings progress.

Try to keep the head still on top of the spine as the weight of the arm is released, resisting the tendency to collapse into the spine on the drop.

Find the continuation of the swing in your imagination at the point of the suspension, the journey continuing into space and beyond. This will help to find free flow and not stop the swing at the top.

Allow the freedom and sensation of the swing to lift your spirits and enjoy.

One arm swing into wide

Progressions:

1   As you swing the right arm across the body, allow the weight to transfer onto your left leg, and back onto right leg as the arm swings back into wide and open. Try not to let the torso twist. Repeat a few times.

2   Progress to allowing the upper body to respond to the motion of the swing and let the shoulders and sternum turn into the direction of the swing, taking your gaze with you and out into the space. Repeat a few times.

3   Add in full circle swings that travel all the way over the top and a change of arm.

4   Progress to swings with a balance at the suspension point: as you swing the right arm across the body, keep your weight centred and body strong. A swing across to closed position, and return again to open, one swing all the way over the top, letting the arm continue across the body and past your head as your weight shifts completely onto the left leg in a balance. Suspend the swing with the balance, the arm reaching out into the space diagonally.

5   Drop the weight back into centre as you allow the arm to swing back to open position once more, repeating the sequence with a balance on the right leg. Repeat as often as desired, letting the momentum of the swing shift your weight and take you effortlessly into a balance.

One arm swing into wide

Use weight of shoulder – use the pull of gravity to release joints.

Think of shoulder doing the movement and leave the arm passive.

Try and find the weight of the shoulder and the arm and allow this weight to help you discover the natural momentum of the swing. It is the releasing of weight, the giving in to gravity, that enables the movement of the swing, not the use of muscle.

Try not to stop the movement at the highest point between each swing, there is a moment of suspension before the journey continues.

The knees must always release on the drop. The knees release as a response to the arm dropping, not in preparation. If the knees remain locked it is hard to find the weight of the swing and experience the release in the shoulder.

It is a small release of the knees at the point of drop in the swing, not a bend of the legs. If the legs engage too much then this also disrupts the natural weight and free flow of the swing.

Have a strong sense of going forwards into space on from the swing and up into space on the circle.

Two arm swing into wide

1   Begin in centre with feet wider than hips.

2   Open both arms out wide in the space to
    shoulder height.

3   Drop the weight of both arms letting them
    swing across the body to a natural suspension,
    then swing back out wide.

4   Repeat as often as desired and progress to full
    circle swings with both arms.

    Progressions:

1   Swing both arms across the body and
    back to open and wide (this is one swing)
    4 times.

2   As the 4th swing opens out into wide shift your
    weight onto the right leg and balance for a
    moment with arms out wide and left leg off the
    floor.

3   Drop the weight back onto both feet and
    continue to swing 4 more times, then balance
    on the left leg with a suspension.

4   Progress to a balance after 2 swings, then after
    1.

5   Progress to dropping the weight of the head
    forwards as the swing closes across the body
    and the head springing back up as the swing
    opens.

One arm swing into wide

Stand with feet well apart and with toes slightly turned out (similar to second position in ballet). Arms by side.

Allow right arm to float away from the body to the side until slightly higher than parallel with the floor. Make sure the arm is to the side and not slightly behind.

Swing the right arm across body and out to the side again. Imagine you have a very heavy dumbbell in your hand. Let the elbow be loose. Allow knees to release as in the other swings.

Repeat about 8 times, repeat with left arm, repeat with both arms.

With one arm repeat with circle overhead, i.e. swing left, swing right, swing over the top.

This can be done in two different patterns, one, finish circle where you started it or two, finish circle on other side so that you can start the sequence on alternate sides.

Now start shifting weight from side to side, this sequence can finish with galloping sideways as you keep swinging the arm.

One arm swing into wide head and sternum release

1 Begin in centre with feet wider than hips, spring the right arm out and up to shoulder height.

2 Let the arm drop and swing across the body and back out to wide, keeping weight centred. Repeat a few times.

3 Progress to the weight shifting through the lower body with the motion of the swing, letting the arm continue past your face, up to your ear and out on a diagonal line. The arm then swings back to wide on the opposite diagonal line. Repeat a few times.

4 On the next swing let the head and sternum release into forward space on the drop of the arm, allowing the head to roll a little with the motion of the swing, returning to a balanced position and looking forwards in the space, as the swing closes across the body and passes by your face once more. Repeat this motion as the arm swings back to wide, with weight shifting and head and sternum releasing.

One arm swing into wide head and sternum release

The weight can shift or remain centred as you swing; shifting requires greater balance and organisation through the body.

As the right arm swings across the body, for example, from right to left, insist the arm travels past the face and suspends directly above the left ear, and the back remains broad without twisting.

You can add in swings over the top to change direction and play with sequencing.

Two arm swing same side

1   Begin in centre with feet wider than hips.

2   Spring both arms out to right side no higher than your shoulder, your right arm will be extending out into wide and the left crossing in front of the body in same direction.

3   Release the weight of both arms and let them swing across the body to the left side then back to the right.

4   Allow the knees to gently respond to the drop of the swing and keep spine long and balanced.

5   Repeat as many times as necessary.

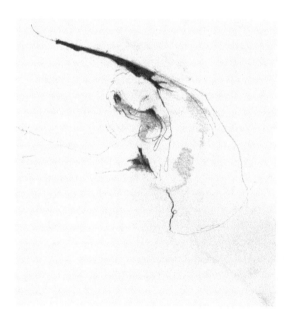

Two arm swing same side

Try to keep your weight slightly forwards from the hips to enable space for both arms to swing freely.

A partner can stand behind the person doing the swing and place both hands on the back of the ribs to encourage an opening and lifting.

Progressions:

1 2 swings across the body, beginning on the right followed by 1 swing continuing all the way over the top and ending to the left side, repeat sequence once more beginning on the left. Let the flow continue between the swings.

2 Transfer your weight between feet with each swing.

3 Release head and sternum on each swing, allowing your upper body to drop into forward space. As the swing travels over to the left side, let the right arm continue up past your head until you are reaching out diagonally with head balancing and torso broad, without twisting. You can choose to keep weight centred through feet or shift it with the swing.

4 Release from the waist or the hips as you swing. Keep the heels grounded in this swing to help you find stability. This is a demanding swing, not for beginners and requires real release, free flow and lots of breath support.

Arm swing forwards and back

1   *Stand with feet together, toes slightly turned out. With left foot take a small step forwards but keep weight evenly distributed between both feet. (Similar to forth position in ballet).*

2   *Raise right arm directly behind you, turning waist a little to allow shoulder to open, palm facing away from body.*

3   *Swing arm forwards and backwards (keeping the direction strictly straight forwards and back) opening shoulder on backward swing. Allow the knees to release as the arm drops (as in diagonal swing). Keep weight firmly distributed between both feet.*

4   *Now swing forwards, back, forwards again and over the head in a circle, returning to back position of arm so that the same movement can be repeated.*

5   *So, swing, forwards, back, forwards and over the top. Repeat 4-8 times.*

6   *Now let weight move forwards and back with the direction of the swing and return to the central position for the circle over the top.*

7   *Repeat with left arm.*

Arm swing forwards and back

Have a strong sense of going forwards into space on from swing and up into space on the circle'

Backhand swing will eventually become less important and more of a preparation'

Always release the knees'

Note. This exercise can finish by continuing with the circle and galloping forwards.

Arm swing on diagonal 'bow and arrow'

1   Begin with right foot in a diagonal stance, feet a little wider than hips and weight evenly balanced.

2   Spring your right arm out and up in front of you to shoulder height, letting the left spring up to join it on a new impulse, palms of both hands facing each other.

3   Sweep your left arm across your chest to open out on the diagonal behind you,
    again at shoulder height, as if you are drawing the string back on a bow. Let the right arm drop to your side so only the
    left remains gesturing out into the space behind you.

4   Let the left arm drop into a swing forwards and backwards in the space, on the diagonal, repeating the swing as many times as desired.

    Progressions:

    You can alternate the swing by circling over the top in both directions. Keep the body strong and balanced, allowing only the arm to have free-flowing movement.

    Progress to transferring the weight between feet, following the motion of the swing.

    Release the head and sternum into forward space on the forward journey of the swing, letting the head and sternum discover balance again as the swing heads into backward space.

Arm swing on diagonal 'bow and arrow'

1 Stand in middle of imaginary square, left foot on slight diagonal in front of right foot (very small step)/

2 Extend left arm to left corner of imaginary square. Bring right hand palm to palm with left hand.

3 Draw right arm back as if pulling on a bow until right hand is at right shoulder. Release right arm to back diagonal as if you have released the arrow. So you are now aligned feet and arms on diagonal.

4 Drop front arm to side. Let right arm swing through from back left corner to the left front corner as if you were swinging a heavy bell (pendulum motion) allowing knees to release on each drop (if the bell is heavy enough, they must do so).

Use the weight of shoulder – use pull of gravity to release joints. Think of shoulder doing the movement and leave the arm passive. Keep head and torso erect.

Leave elbow loose. Open your shoulder when you swing back. You may turn your head towards back to check; also, it will feel more comfortable when you first do this exercise.

Think of your shoulder blade as the motor for the action so as to get the fullest release and heaviest movement. Isolate the movement to arm and shoulder.

Two arm swing forwards in opposition

1   Begin in centre, feet hip width apart.

2   Reach the left arm forwards in the space to
    shoulder height and the right arm behind you
    into backward space, allowing the torso to twist
    from the hips and the right shoulder to open,
    palm facing outwardly.

4   Swing both arms forwards and backwards at
    the same time in opposite directions to each
    other, letting the knees respond to the drop of
    each swing and the spine stay long and stable.

5   Repeat as often as desired.

6   Progress to the swings travelling over the top in
    a circular motion, both arms in opposite
    directions to each other, to a beat of 1, 2, over
    the top and out. This allows for the over-the-top
    swing to travel in both directions.

Two arm swing forwards in opposition

This swing can begin with a forwards and back motion in opposition without a twist through the torso, the shoulders remaining flat to the front.

After 4 or 8 swings the body twists, allowing the shoulder of the arm swinging into backward space to open and take up more space.

Repeat this for another 4 or 8 swings.

Try to sustain full length and breadth through the spine during this swing, resisting any wobble in the torso and the head remaining balanced.

Two arm swing forwards in opposition 'monkey swing'

1   Begin in centre, feet hip width apart.

2   Bend into the knees and tip the upper body forwards in the space from the hips, keeping the spine long and broad and the head following the line of the spine.

3   Reach the left arm forwards in the space to shoulder height and the right arm behind you into backward space, keeping the elbow soft, palm facing inwards, and the arm at a height that does not require any lifting of the shoulder. Keep shoulders flat to the front.

4   Swing both arms forwards and backwards at the same time in opposite directions to each other, letting the knees respond to the drop of each swing or every other swing. Try not to twist the upper body and keep the spine as long and stable as possible.

5   Repeat as often as desired.

6   Continue the swing of both arms allowing the momentum of the swing to lift your weight off your heels and onto the balls of your feet. Try not to lose contact with the ground. Allow your heels to return to the ground on the drop of every swing so you are essentially bouncing up and down on to the balls of the feet, or on the drop of every other swing.

Two arm swing forwards in opposition 'monkey swing' (continued)

7   Repeat for 8 swings.

8   Continue the swing of both arms in opposition allowing the momentum of the swing to lift your weight off both feet with a little jump, a spring away from the floor, returning to the ground with the drop of each swing or every other swing.

9   Repeat as often as desired.

Progressions:

1   Swing both arms in opposition for 8 counts, tipping forwards from the hips with a long flat spine.

2   Continue the motion of the swing and let the head and sternum release into forward space so the head is hanging for 8 counts.

3   Continue the motion of the swing and let the torso drop all the way down, releasing from the hips, allowing the spine to respond to the natural momentum of the swing, undulating effortlessly whilst swinging both arms in opposition. Repeat for 8 swings, letting the rebound of the 8th swing spring you back up to standing with one arm reaching up into high space.

Two arm swing forwards in opposition 'monkey swing'

Allow the momentum of the swing to lift your body off the ground. If you connect to the weight of the arms then the swing will be the impulse for the rise or the jump.

The position of your upper body is very important in this swing. Try to lean forwards from the hips and not the waist, keeping your spine as flat as possible. Do not arch or round into the spine.

This swing requires a strong spine so should not be taught to beginners. For beginners do not tip so far forwards.

Find the freedom and weight in the swing as a gorilla does when swinging their arms.

Sustain the position through your upper body, trying not to let the upper spine rotate in the direction of the arm.

Play with the sense of travelling forwards. Let the freedom in the movement inspire you and this will encourage the release and the spring.

Two arm swing forwards in opposition 'monkey swing'

Try to maintain alignment and space through the lower body; resist the knees rolling in on the landing of the jump. Keep the feet in parallel and the knees directly over the toes and below the hips.

The progression of this swing into a full body swing requires a big release of breath and weight, if there is any holding then the body will be under strain. Enjoy the natural flow and momentum of the swing into the natural undulation of the spine.

Use the rebound motion following the drop to bring yourself all the way up to standing at the end of the body swing section, with one arm reaching up into high space and the other arm hanging by your side, or you can repeat the sequence of swings from here, tipping the body forwards once again.

Two arm swing forward 'ski swing'

1 Begin in centre with feet slightly narrower than hips width apart.

2 Bend into the knees and tip the upper body slightly forwards in the space from the hips, keeping the spine long and broad and the head following the line of the spine.

3 Reach both arms forwards and up to shoulder height, keeping elbows soft and hands gesturing on into space.

4 Let both arms swing backwards and forwards in the space at the same time, and only up to a comfortable height in backward space so as not to lift the shoulders.

5 Repeat the swing as often as desired, encouraging the spine to stay long and broad and the upper body tipped forwards.

6 Continue the swing of both arms, allowing the momentum of the swing to lift your weight off your heels and onto the balls of your feet. Try not to lose contact with the ground. Allow your heels to return to the ground on the drop of every swing so you are essentially bouncing up and down on to the balls of the feet, or on the drop of every other swing.

Two arm swing forward 'ski swing' (continued)

7 Repeat for 8 swings.

8 Continue the swing of both arms in opposition, allowing the momentum of the swing to lift your weight off both feet with a little jump, a spring away from the floor, returning to the ground with the drop of each swing or every other swing.

9 Repeat as often as desired.

Progression:

1 After 4 swings with the torso tipped slightly forwards and feet grounded, let the weight of the torso release forwards and down into a body swing for 4 counts, both arms swinging backwards and forwards as the spine drops, rebounds and naturally undulates.

2 After the 4th body swing let the momentum of the swing bring you all the way up to standing with both arms above your head, spine long and body balanced. Enjoy the suspension here for a moment then slowly bring arms out wide into the space and back down to sides.

3 Or repeat the sequence of swings once again, beginning with 4 swings with a balanced body, 4 with the torso tipped forwards slightly and dropping into 4 body swings.

Two arm swing forward 'ski swing'

Try to insist on full length and breadth of the back throughout the swing when you are tipped forwards in the space. It is challenging to sustain this but try to resist the spine collapsing with the weight of the swing.

Insist that the head stays in line with the spine, resist the temptation to look forwards in space which will tip the head up and put pressure on the neck.

Let the knees respond to the drop in the swing.

When releasing into the body swing, connect to the weight of the head to begin with then progress to getting the whole spine involved and undulating.

Swings

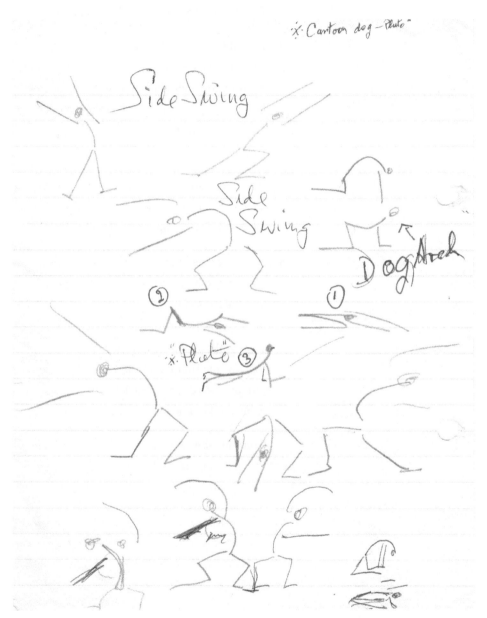

Notes by Trish Arnold. Courtesy author's personal archive.

Two arm swing one forwards one wide

1   Begin in centre with feet wider than hips.

2   Shift the weight onto the right leg, leaving the toes of the left foot connected to the ground to support you. Lengthen and bend your upper body over to the right a little, keeping the torso flat towards the front and letting the arms hang freely.

3   Reach forwards with the right arm raising it to shoulder height and at the same time raise the left arm out wide, again, at shoulder height.

4   Drop the weight of both arms into a swing, the right swinging forwards and back in the space and the left swinging across the body and back out to wide. Allow the knee to release with the drop of the swings and the torso twist slightly to allow the shoulder of the right arm to open into backward space. The left foot remains connected to the floor.

5   Continue the swing with both arms, enjoying the sensation of sending energy forwards and out into the space through both arms.

6   Play with breath and sound, adding in a 'hey' as you swing into forward and wide space. Repeat as many times as desired and then on the other side.

Two arm swing one forwards one wide

Progression:

1   Build up the momentum of the swing
    until you feel the free foot lift off the floor
    in the suspension of the swing when one arm is
    forwards and the other out in
    wide. The foot returns to the ground to balance
    the body as the arms swing backwards and
    across the body. Repeat
    for 4 or 8 swings.

2   Using the momentum of the swing, lift the free
    leg off the floor entirely and bring the foot and
    ankle to rest behind the standing leg at calf
    height as the arms swing backwards and across
    the body, letting the leg return out to wide as the
    swing opens out into forwards and wide. Keep
    the weight off the floor in a balance on one leg
    and repeat the swing for 4 or 8.

Try to insist the torso remains at its full length
and breadth, resisting any collapse through the
spine as you swing.

The knee of the standing leg responds to the
weight of the swing with a little release on the
moment of the drop.

Figure of 8 arm swing in wide

1 Begin in centre with feet wider than your hips.

2 Draw a figure of 8 on its side in front of the body with the right hand, increasing the size of the 8 as you go until you feel the second half of the figure of 8 curving around your body to the side and out behind you.

3 When the figure of 8 has reached its full size into high and low space, discover the weight of the arm and release into the swing, the right arm swinging flat across the body and up into high space then opening out into backward space behind you.

3 Repeat the swing a few times, following the journey of the swing with your gaze and beginning to allow the head and sternum to release into the lowest closed part of the figure of 8 and the head and sternum to lift and open into the highest backward point.

4 Repeat with the other arm.

Figure of 8 arm swing in wide

Roll both shoulders in a figure of 8 motion and repeat a few times.

Place both hands onto the shoulders and draw figure of 8 with your elbows, allowing the upper spine to get a little more involved, rounding and arching through the upper spine.

If you allow the gaze to follow the swing then the upper spine begins to get involved, the sternum closing on the forward swing and opening on the backward swing.

Really find the drop, the release into gravity, then the discovery of the up, the high space, is effortless.

This swing can develop until the whole of the upper body is involved, the pelvis undulates forwards as the arm swings into backwards space.

Try to find a balance in the closing and opening of the body with the swing.

Trish Arnold would encourage actors to say '*Imprisonment, liberation*' during this swing, as the body closed and opened into the space.

Figure of 8 arm swing in wide

Progression:

This figure of 8 swing can be repeated with both arms.

1   Begin in centre with feet wider than hips, spring both arms out wide up to shoulder height.

2   Release the weight of both arms, letting them swing down across the body and back up into high space. Both arms then release down once more and travel out past the sides of the body into backwards space and back up into high, to repeat the journey once more.

3   As you progress with the swing, allow the torso to become more involved, dropping forwards from the sternum as the swing closes in front of you, and letting the pelvis come forwards into an undulation as the arms open out behind you.

This is a physically demanding swing so do not do too many and not recommended for beginners.

Engage the breath and play with sound to encourage free flow and an effortless, natural connection with gravity.

Swings

Pendulum.

6. Diagonal Swing

Imagine you are standing in the middle of a square.
Move your left foot forward so that standing on a diagonal
line from corner N¡. to corner N°. 3.
Extend ~~the~~ the left arm forward to corner N° 3.
Bring the right hand to left hand palm to palm.
Draw the right hand backwards along the inside of L. arm
and across the chest and out to corner N° 1.
as if you are pulling an arrow from the bow and releasing
it finishing with your arm in the diagonal line
from 1 to 3.
You are now standing with your feet + arms on the
diagonal.

Drop the front arm. (Left.)
Swing the R. arm forward + back on that diagonal.
as if you were swinging a heavy bell. (pendulum)
ALLOW YOUR KNEES to RELEASE as the arm drops.
(If the bell is heavy enough they must do so!)

Think of your shoulder blade as the motor for the action so
as to get the fullest release + easiest movement.
Isolate the movement to arm + shoulder.
Keep head and torso erect.
Leave elbow loose.
Open shoulder when you swing to the back.
You may turn your head towards back to check — do it
feels more comfortable when you first do this exercise.
Repeat swing for 16 counts 1 + 2 + etc.
Repeat on other ~~side~~ diagonal.

P.T.O.

Notes by Trish Arnold. Courtesy author's personal archive.

Figure of 8 arm swing on diagonal

1   Begin in centre with feet at hips width, step into your right diagonal with the right foot slightly turned out. Imagine you are standing in a cube with the right foot following in the direction of the right diagonal of the cube and you left foot following the left diagonal of the cube.

2   Draw a small figure of 8 on its side with your left hand in front of your body, increasing the size of the figure of 8 as you go until you feel the first part of the 8 travel down into your left diagonal and up into high space and the second part of the 8 curve around your torso into backward space.

3   Discover the weight of the arm as you release into the swing, allowing the drop to help you discover the highest point of the swing in space; the forward swing travels down and out on the right diagonal and the backward swing travels down and out on the left diagonal behind you, reaching into the right back corner.

4   Repeat the swing as many times as desired and enjoy the sensation of closing and opening through the upper body, particularly the sternum, letting your gaze follow the movement of the hand.

5   Repeat with the other arm, stepping into the left diagonal with the left foot.

Figure of 8 arm swing on diagonal

Figure of 8 swing: begin with small 8 with hand and wrist in front. Extend shape. Use hand to draw 8 moving to side, see curve in 8 bending round. Both arms then drop in front.

Connect to the drop of the arm from deep in the shoulder and let this help you find the height of the swing.

Always use back arm. Swing comes from shoulder, turning in. Always follows lift in body.

Forehand backhand swing with one arm

1 Begin in centre with feet wider than hips. Spring the left arm out into wide at shoulder height, then take it a little further back into the space behind you.

2 Let the arm release down and forwards into a swing as though you are hitting a tennis ball with a forehand stroke, discovering the suspension of the swing directly in front of you.

3 The second part of the swing travels past your left side as though you are hitting a tennis ball with a backhand stroke.

4 Repeat as many times as desired, enjoying the drop into the forehand and backhand swing and letting the swing travel out into the space. Play with adding sounds and words.

Arm swings with gallops

1   Begin standing in centre, in the back left corner of a large space with your right shoulder facing the diagonal journey across the space.

2   Spring the left arm out wide at shoulder height and shift the weight slightly onto your left leg.

3   Gallop across the room on the diagonal as you swing your left arm across the body and back out to wide, keeping the back at its full length and breadth and head balanced on top of the spine.

4   Add in two or three full circle swings over the top if you have the space and let a 'hey' spring out of the body at the same time.

5   Repeat the swing with a gallop on the other diagonal of the room and with the right arm, left shoulder facing the direction of travel.

Progressions:

1   Repeat the swings and gallops with both arms opening out to begin and closing and opening across the body as you gallop.

2   Repeat the swing with both arms swinging across the body in the same direction, beginning with the arms gesturing away from the direction of travel at shoulder height.

Arm swings with gallops

There are many variations of swings across the space with a gallop; using one arm, both arms, with actors passing each other from either diagonal in the space, facing each other in pairs, or coming from all four corners of a room, for example. Just let yourself play with the many possibilities.

Enjoy letting the momentum of the swing carry you and play with the relationship with space and the others around you.

Try to keep the spine long whilst galloping and swinging the arms, resisting the arms opening out too far past your peripheral vision as this weakens the body, disconnects the breath and voice by closing the space in between the shoulders.

Forehand backhand swing with gallops

1　Begin in the corner of the space with right shoulder facing the direction of travel across the diagonal, feet wider than hips. Spring the left arm out wide to shoulder height.

2　The left arm releases and swings in continuous full circles throughout, beginning with a forehand swing (as though you are hitting a tennis ball) at the same time as you gallop across the space.

3　After 2 gallops you change direction, the body turning 180 degrees around your right shoulder, mid gallop, the arm continuing its flow of the swing in a full circle but has changed to a backhand stroke.

4　This continues across the space; the arm swinging one and a half full circles in forehand and backhand direction and the galloping continuing with a half turn after every 2 gallops.

5　Repeat on the other diagonal and with the right arm beginning out wide at shoulder height and the left shoulder facing the direction of travel.

Forehand backhand swing with gallops

Try to let the flow of the swing continue; it is the body that changes direction and the journey of the arm swing continues. Because you have changed direction the swing does too but without interruption to the flow.

Try to sustain full length and breadth through the back during the swing, a strong centre that enables you to feel the free flow of the shifting swing.

Progressions:

You can play with this swing in pairs facing each other to begin with, turning away from each other and then finding each other throughout the journey of the swings and gallops.

You can slow this swing down so it is more of a step than a gallop and do one full circle before changing direction.

Body swing 'elephant swing'

1   Begin in centre with feet a little narrower than
    hips. Release the weight of the head and let it
    take you down through the spine until you are
    hanging from the pelvis with long legs and soft
    knees.

2   Reach out both arms in front of you into
    forward space, lifting the head and the torso
    and following your gesture with your gaze.

3   Drop the weight of the body and arms on an
    exhalation and notice the rebound motion that
    occurs naturally as you surrender the weight of
    the body.

4   Reach into backward space with both arms,
    lifting the torso and head a little so you have
    somewhere to drop from.

5   Drop the weight of the body and arms on an
    exhalation.

6   Reach out once more into forward space with
    both arms, seeing into the space in front, then
    let go of the weight of the body allowing the
    arms to swing backwards and forwards, with
    the torso naturally responding to the swing and
    the head hanging freely.

7   Repeat as many times as desired. Uncurl slowly
    to standing.

Body swing 'elephant swing'

Try to honestly let go of the weight of the head in this swing; the movement of the head and body is a response to the natural momentum of the swing.

As the body discovers the natural momentum of the swing and releases into gravity, the spine will find an effortless undulation. This can be encouraged as the swing develops.

Think of the weight of an elephant and the ease as it swings its trunk.

Connect to the breath and sound as you swing.

Progressions:

Repeat the swing 4 or 8 times forwards and backwards then let the rebound of the swing send you up to standing with arms above your head. Really let yourself find the drop and the rebound, the discovery of high space is then effortless.

Full torso swing 'tree toppling'

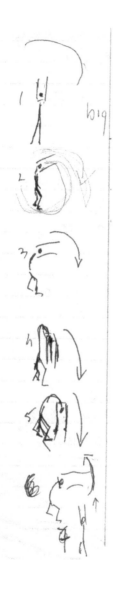

1   Begin in centre with feet a little narrower than
    hip distance apart.

2   Spring both arms out wide and up into
    high space on an impulse with an
    effortless inhalation, palms facing
    forwards.

3   Keeping the back long and broad and the whole
    body straight like a tree trunk with heels rooted
    into the earth, shift your weight forwards and
    out as though you are about to fall off a cliff.

4   When you can go no further let yourself
    fall forwards, keeping the heels rooted. Connect
    to the momentum of the fall, release into the
    weight of the body, letting go of the head, arms
    and body and follow the journey of the swing
    all the way down. The arms swing behind you,
    then drop again into gravity and rebound all
    the way back up into high space with the arms
    reaching up to the sky.

5   Suspend at the top for a moment, enjoying the
    exhilaration and possibilities, then bring both
    arms out slowly to wide space and down.

6   Repeat as many times as desired.

Full torso swing 'tree toppling'

Arms embrace wide space to come up into swing. Alternately they can spring up through centre of body.

Full torso swing. Can use direct journey up with arms because this is on the wheel plane.

When arms are in high space, release the shoulders and keep length through back of the neck, gaze forwards in space to help this.

Try to take the pelvis with you into the swing, holding on to the image of a tree toppling from its roots. This will help the pelvis to shift forwards and the whole body remain long and straight. (If the body bends from the hips into the swing, it is impossible to discover the same dramatic release and fullness of swing, the spine consequently arches down rather than remaining long and the sense of risk is lost.)

Tip forwards into the swing as if about to fall off a cliff edge.

The sense of forward motion is more important than down.

The dramatic story of this swing is the moment of risk, release, then suspension, the moment before you speak. And letting the breath and voice play a part in these moments.

Full torso swing 'tree toppling'

Warm up for full torso: Drop over, take arms behind you slightly, lift on 'and', 4 swings with no body moving, 8 swings with progression as body rises slightly, on 8th come up to full height and into full torso.

Try to really connect to the drop, the release of weight and breath and the consequent rebound; it is this moment that enables you to return to your full height with effortlessness.

Resist the temptation to push your way up. Use the natural momentum of the swing and the honest weight of the body. Try to leave yourself alone.

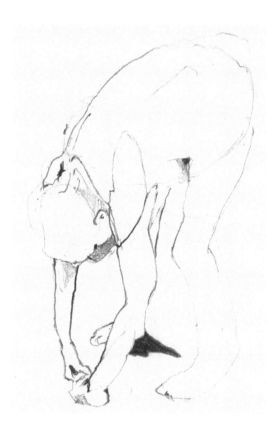

Full torso swing 'tree toppling'

Progressions:

1   Can add in bounces in knees before swing or after swing.

2   Instead of coming straight back up, let the body swing for 2 or 4 more full swings forwards and backwards.

3   Twist upper body onto right diagonal and swing over right leg and up, repeat on other diagonal playing with balance and space.

Don't focus on the arch going down, it has to be a fall.

The undulation in the spine happens after the initial drop.

Torso swing to sides

1   Begin in centre, feet much wider than your hips.

2   Release the head and roll down through the spine so you are hanging freely out of the pelvis with knees released.

3   Keeping the weight balanced between both feet, send your arms and torso out to the left, lifting the body and head to just below waist height as you go and reaching out with both arms, gaze following your gesture.

4   Release the weight of the torso, head and arms and swing the body to the right, letting it swing up as high as the momentum takes you, about waist height again.

5   Repeat a few times swinging side to side.

6   Let the swing come back to stillness hanging in the centre and uncurl slowly up to your full height.

Torso swing to sides

Try to let the weight of the head go during this swing.

Keep weight centred and knees very responsive to the drop of the swing, resisting temptation to sit back in heels.

The more the weight is forwards through the front of your feet with the heels grounded, the more you will experience the full release of the swing.

Let the breath release with the swing and progress to releasing sound as you drop and swing, it will help you to connect to the weight of the body.

Progression:

Once you have discovered the freedom and release in this swing you can progress to letting the spine become more involved, finding the natural undulation at the sides as the body changes direction. This undulation begins with the tail and ripples through the spine into an arch.

Torso swing to sides and over the top

1 Begin in centre, feet much wider than your hips. Release the head and roll down through the spine so you are hanging out of the pelvis with knees released.

2 Keeping the weight balanced between both feet, send your arms and torso to the left, lifting the body and head to just below waist height as you go and reaching out with both arms.

4 Release the weight of the torso, head and arms and swing the body to the right, letting it swing up as high as the momentum takes you, about waist height again.

5 Repeat a few times swinging side to side and as you swing into wide begin to open the top shoulder so you are starting to face forwards in this moment and less on a diagonal.

6 Repeat this a few times swinging a little higher each time.

7 Feel the progression through breath and body and let the momentum of the swing take you all the way over the top through high space and drop back through wide on the other side. Let the swing come back to stillness hanging in the centre and uncurl slowly up to your full height.

Torso swing to sides and over the top

As with all body swings, try to release the weight of the head. Any tension in the neck will inhibit the free flow of a natural swing. This is a big movement, but it is a far less strenuous one if you breathe and really let go of the weight of the body.

Connect to high space when swinging over the top.

It is the drop that allows you to find the height; the more honestly you connect to the drop, the more committed the connection to high space will be.

Notice how the natural momentum of the swing slows down as it reaches the sides and the top, at the sides as it changes direction, and at the top before the body falls into gravity.

Progression:

You can begin this swing by reaching to the side and opening out the top shoulder at the start of the swing, so the body is flat to the front instead of building up to this point. It is advisable to come up a little further at the side if you are to start flat as it is a big movement through the torso.

Two arm swing with undulation

1   Begin in centre with feet wider than your hips.

2   Spring both arms out wide to shoulder height.

3   Release both arms to swing across the body; the spine arches and the torso releases all the way down at the same time.

4   The drop of the torso is followed by the rebound and the spine rounds up halfway as the arms swing across the body, the spine then arches all the way down once more, as the arms change direction and begin the journey towards swinging open.

5   There is another drop of the torso, leading into the rebound movement as the spine rounds all the way up to the top and the arms continue their swing out wide.

6   *Repeat a few times then rest in a squat position or standing quietly.*

```
b) From wide stance
   1. Swing arms across body
   2. Swing arms to wide
   3. Swing down torso and head (w. undulating back)
   4. Swing up to wide

   Variation    Add balance on toes
                or stay down for counts 2 and 3, up on 4

   FINISH EXERCISE STANDING QUIETLY.
```

Notes by Trish Arnold. Courtesy author's personal archive.

Two arm swing with undulation

Wide stance through the legs to encourage grounding and support, with knees that respond and release to the drop of the swing. Try not to let the knees bend too much as this takes away the fullness of the drop and rebound.

Encourage the tail to begin the journey of the arched spine, both at the beginning of the swing and during the undulation. The spine ripples through into an arch from tail to head.

It is important to really connect to the weight of the torso and the head, to discover the drop and the rebound, as this is the impulse for the undulation through the spine, letting go of the weight and the breath at the same time.

It is a very dynamic and bold swing that requires much preparation, but it is also worth remembering that the movement through the spine is a very natural journey if the connection to weight is found.

Two arm swing into lunge swing 'martial art swing'

1 Begin in centre, feet much wider than hips. Both arms spring open wide to shoulder height.

2 Release the weight of both arms into a swing across the body and return to wide and open, releasing the knees at the moment of the drop.

3 Repeat 4 times. As you finish the fourth swing, rotate body a quarter turn to left into a lunge stance; left foot pointing forwards in the space, left knee bent, right foot pointing in same direction with ball of foot into the floor, heel lifted and right leg straight but not locked. Your left arm will now be reaching into forward space and your right behind you in backward space with the right shoulder rotating in, palm of the hand facing inwards.

5 Swing both arms forwards and backwards in lunge position, letting knees respond to the drop.

Heel dropping at back and a stretch on each swing.

6 Repeat 4 times. As you finish the fourth swing, a quarter turn to your right to face your original front once more with both arms out wide.

7 Repeat swing in wide for 4 then quarter turn to the right for 4 lunge swings.

Two arm swing into lunge swing 'martial art swing'

Use the free-flowing motion of the swing to encourage the quarter turns through the body.

Notice the rotation through the torso in the lunge swing.

Enjoy the inward/outward rotation of the hip as you turn into/out of the lunge swing (the right hip as you turn to the left, the left hip as you turn to the right).

Progress to 2 swings instead of 4.

Remember the rhythm and say 'Drop' to encourage the swing.

Powerful swing, facing someone creates challenges.

Leg swings

Leg swings use the natural dynamic of gravity to release any habitual tension in the pelvic area, hips and lower spine. They create more space and ease of motion, using weight to lengthen and open the hip flexors. Similar to an arm or torso swing, leg swings connect to the dynamic of drop and rebound, and free flow, followed by a moment of suspension before the swing repeats. The relationship between the movement of the pelvis and the journey of your leg is a focal point. It is the swing of the leg that leads you into walk; the freer this motion, the more free and open your walk will be, as you contact your natural length of stride without physical inhibition.

Variations to the upright leg swings can be explored by lying on your side with the top leg swinging freely out into the space in front and behind your torso.

Puppet kicks

1 Stand with feet in a relaxed first position, slightly turned out, heels close but not touching.

2 Throw the right leg out to the side with the impulse coming from the knee, on a diagonal angle to the body, the leg swings out off the floor as high as you desire with a loose ankle and foot.

3 At the same time spring up on the left foot.

4 The right leg returns to central stance as the left leg is thrown out to the side.

5 Repeat for as many as required.

Begin without the jumps and just throw the leg out into the space to find the release and freedom of the movement in the hip, knee and ankle joints, then progress to adding in a jump.

These are light, loose, springy jumps that help release into the hips and soften the legs, and are often explored before leg swings.

Think of a puppet, the torso remains strong and balanced, it is just the leg that swings freely from the hips. Let the arms hang freely and respond naturally to the movement.

Forward leg swing

1   Begin by holding onto a bar, the back of a chair or a partner's shoulder on your right side with your right hand. Stand with feet narrow and parallel.

2   Using your free arm, scoop the left leg up in front of you so the upper leg is at a right angle with the torso and the lower leg and foot are hanging freely. Release the hand and let the arm hang freely by your side, lengthening through the spine and checking the standing leg is braced; long and strong with no bend in the knee.

3   Let go of the weight of the left leg and let it swing down to the floor and into backward space, making sure both hips are pointing forwards, the left hip is not turning out and that the knee of the left leg is facing the floor.

4   Continue with the swing as the leg changes direction and returns to forward space. Repeat as many times as desired.

5   Finish the swing in forward space with a suspension, then place the foot on the floor slightly wider than hips. Notice the space through the body.

6   Turn round and use your left hand to support you and scoop up the right leg. Repeat the swing on this side as often as desired.

Forward leg swing

Try to keep the standing leg braced throughout so there is room enough for the other leg to swing freely and the ankle to remain released. If the standing leg releases then the instinct is to protect the leg that is swinging by tensing thus hindering the swing.

Try to keep the ankle and the foot as released as possible, the foot falls flat on the floor during the swing and slides along in parallel on both the forward and backward journey of the swing.

The release comes from deep in the hip socket.

Notice the natural arching and rounding of the pelvis as this is what enables the leg to swing freely. Try to keep the upper body balanced and centred with your weight remaining forwards over the standing leg and not too influenced by the swing of the free leg.

Think of the leg lengthening away from you in both directions during the swing; this encourages the leg to swing freely with space and a sense of direction rather than drawing the leg in and up.

Lift leg, slap knee with hand to drop knee, go into swing, focus on swing.

Take foot behind (ankle) and stretch then drop, then focus on hip and lower spine motion.

Place hand on lower spine, awareness of how body works and movement in the spine and hips.

Forward leg swing

Progressions:

1 Begin with leg in backward space, lifted and extended out behind you, to experience the tilt in the pelvis and the knee and hip remaining aligned. Swing the leg as many times as desired.

2 Finish the swing in forward space and place foot down in centre.

3 Begin with leg lifted in forward space. After swinging the leg for 8 beats, one beat being a backward and backward swing, drop onto the front leg into a low lunge.

4 Spring back up into a balance and repeat swing or spring forwards on to the other foot and swing with this leg

   The above swing can be done in the space and not using a partner or the wall to help balance.

5 Instead of dropping into a lunge, let the leg drop to the ground after 2 swings in front of the standing leg; the head and sternum drop forwards and over at the same time, and bounce through the knees for 4 beats with weight balanced between both legs. Spring up into a balance once more on the 4th beat to repeat the 2 leg swings.

Forward leg swing

Progression:

1   Begin in centre with feet in narrow and scoop
up the right leg into forward space. At the same
time spring the left arm forwards and the right
arm behind you. Do not turn out the back
shoulder, keep the palm of the hands facing
inwards.

2   Let the arms swing with the leg swing,
as if walking in space. This is a low, gentle arm
swing into forward and backward space
following the natural motion of the leg swing
with the body working in opposition.

Keep the length through the spine and resist the
torso rotating with the swing of the arms.

Let the breath flow freely with your gaze forwards
in the space, looking out as though travelling
forwards.

Wide leg swing

1   Begin by holding onto a bar, the back of a chair or a partner's shoulder on your left side with your left hand. Stand with feet narrow and parallel.

2   Using your free arm, scoop the right leg up in front of you so the upper leg is a little lower than a right angle with the torso and the lower leg and foot hanging freely.

3   Release the hand and let the arm hang freely by your side, lengthening through the spine and checking the standing leg is braced; long and strong with no bend in the knee.

4   Open the right hip and leg out into wide, keeping the lower leg and foot hanging freely.

5   Let go of the weight of the leg and let it drop down to the floor and into a swing, the hip rotating inwards as it passes in front of the standing leg and swings freely into wide on the other side with the hip in a closed position. Let the swing continue back to the starting position of open and wide.

6   Repeat as often as required and end the swing with your feet a little wider than hips.

Wide leg swing

This swing is not advisable for beginners as it requires an honest and committed relationship to the drop of weight into gravity and can cause strain in the hip socket if carried out with tension.

This is a big swing for the hips, so it is advisable not to do too many.

Try to maintain full length and breadth through the torso during the swing, keeping as balanced as possible and not moving too much with the movement of the leg.

It is vital to really drop the weight of the leg in this swing; the rotation in the hip needs to happen in the moment of release.

Think of lengthening the leg out into wide space, swinging away from the hips/torso; this helps the lower leg to stay released and respond to the motion of the swing.

This swing travels from side to side with no figure of 8 motion; it is a dropping of weight and a rotation.

Wide leg swing

Progressions:

1   Begin in centre, standing unsupported in the space, spring the right leg up in front and out into wide space. At the same time spring both arms out wide.

2   As you swing the right leg closed across the body and back out to wide, let both arms swing across the body and back out to open and wide at the same time. Repeat for 4 or 8 swings.

3   Suspend in wide with leg and arms open for a moment, then drop into a wide lunge, taking the left arm over your head reaching out into the space, keeping the body flat to the front.

4   Spring back up onto the left leg as arms open out wide once more and repeat the swing.

5   Repeat on the other side.

    Try not to let the torso twist with the swing of the arms and the rotation of the hip, sustain the body facing forwards at all times with the back long and broad.

    This is a challenging swing and not recommended for beginners. Use the breath to support the body.

Leg swings

Class

Leg Swings

① A. Swings on steep plane (forward + back)
B. " " " into forward lunge.
C. " " " " " " + balance back onto
supporting leg.

2. A. Swings on flat plane
B. Into side lunge + balance back onto supporting leg.
C. " " " + side bend, armover
then balance back onto supporting leg.

③ 'Eight swings' Figure of eight develop to full swing which
includes torso & head. Weight & lightness overhead.

Notes by Trish Arnold. Courtesy author's personal archive.

Figure of 8 leg swing

1 Begin in centre with feet wider than hip distance, feet slightly off parallel, arms hanging by your side.

2 Bring both arms out into wide to help with balance, or hold on to a partner's shoulder, back of a chair or a wall, maintaining a long, stable spine.

3 Spring the right leg up from the knee, opening the leg into wide, letting the lower leg and foot hang freely.

4 Draw a figure of 8 with your knee, the centre of the 8 being directly in front of your body, the second half of the 8 is on the left side of the body with the hip in a closed position.

5 Discover the weight of the leg and the drop into gravity as you swing the leg in the figure of 8; the drop is at the centre of the figure of 8 as the hip rotates from open to closed and back to open.

6 Repeat a few times, bringing the foot back down to the ground into a wide stance at the end and standing still for a moment to notice the consequence of the swing.

7 Repeat with the left leg.

Figure of 8 leg swing

It is best to practise this swing holding on to someone's shoulder, a wall, or the back of a chair to help with balance before progressing into standing unsupported in the space.

This swing leads from the hip; the hip is closing and opening, rotating in the hip socket.

Allow the lower part of the leg and the ankle and foot to hang freely and move in response to the movement of the hip.

Really find the release in the swing; try to work with a drop of weight, otherwise there will be tension in the swing and this will cause strain on the hip.

Do not do too many as this is a big swing and a lot of work into the hips.

Keep the swing low and heavy and the spine stable and still, resisting any twisting through the torso with the movement of the leg.

Figure of 8 leg swing

Progression:

1   Holding on to the wall or the back of a chair for
    support, spring the left leg out wide and the left
    arm out into wide at shoulder height.

2   Let the leg drop into the figure of 8 leg swing
    and after 2 full swings release the left arm and
    follow the journey into a figure of 8 arm swing
    at the same time as the leg. The arm and leg
    close and open at the same time.

3   Repeat for 4 or 8 swings, bringing the leg and
    arm back to centre at the end.

4   Change direction in the space and repeat with
    the right arm and leg.

    No need to let the torso undulate or twist much
    in this swing, just enjoy the opening and closing
    dynamic.

    Your gaze can follow the journey of the arm
    swing, encouraging the sternum to get more
    involved in the movement.

    This is a big swing and not recommended for
    beginners. Use plenty of free-flowing breath to
    support the body.

Four

Interviews and Writings

———

The Movement Work Today

Photographs by Stanley Morgan, © Stanley Morgan, 2022. Taken during a private movement workshop organised by Lizzie Ballinger at RADA, London, for graduate actors from LAMDA and RADA. From top left, clockwise: Daniel Bowerbank, Lizzie Ballinger, Lizzie Ballinger, Sam Stafford, Harvey Comerford (just seen).

From top left, clockwise: Ian Bouillion, Sam Stafford, Lizzie Ballinger, Elizabeth Hollingshead.

From top left, clockwise: **Daniel Bowerbank, Sam Stafford, Harvey Comerford, Lizzie Ballinger, Daniel Bowerbank, Lizzie Ballinger, Sam Stafford, Ian Bouillion.**

From left, clockwise: Lizzie Ballinger, Eric Sirakian, Eric Sirakian, Daniel Bowerbank, Lizzie Ballinger.

Interviews and writings

———

This final chapter brings together a range of interviews and discussions about the movement practice from those engaging with the work today. It felt necessary to connect with voices other than my own to allow a different perspective, to hear how it moves others and how the work has evolved. Scattered in between the interviews are testimonials from professional actors I have trained and students still working with me.

On previous pages, I have focused on how this practice is used within an actor training environment, and yet it effortlessly extends into professional theatre and film situations, because the foundations of Pure Movement support all creative circumstances. In the classroom, I am hoping to draw out the student's own range and connection. As a Movement Director, I am responding to the specific needs of the text, the character and the director's vision, and then offering proposals that elicit the actor's relationship to these dynamics. To be clear, it is not the same as choreography, although some choreography might be used as an additional tool if applicable. The work into the world of the play has more pace and direction than teaching, while still accommodating space for the actor's sensation and imagination. The principal dynamics of release and tension, opening and closing, free flow and suspension can illuminate any play, bringing vitality and clarity into the physical instrument of an actor's body.

An example of this can be found in the first interview below, discussing Jane Gibson's Movement Directing work, and her exploration of flow in space. It is a vital aspect of the work of a Movement Director using this practice.

Declan Donnellan – Artistic Director Cheek By Jowl

———

I begin with an interview by Declan Donnellan, Artistic Director of Cheek By Jowl. Declan and his partner Nic Ormerod have been working with Jane Gibson for over thirty years; Jane is an Associate Director of the company. I sent Declan a few questions regarding Jane's involvement in their productions. Having worked with Cheek By Jowl myself and witnessed first-hand the collaboration in the space, I was curious to hear Declan's view on what it is that Jane brings to his work.

Lizzie: How did you meet Jane Gibson and when?

Declan: We were first introduced to Jane in 1988 for our first show at the national. Our first play was *Fuente Ovejune* by Lope De Vega. We wanted to use dance and invited Jane to help. The actors were terrific, we all worked hard, and the opening night went very well. We were invited to perform it in Spain, at the Lope de Vega theatre in Seville. We were all very excited but on the plane I remember feeling suddenly nervous about the prospect of English actors dancing flamenco in Andalusia. On that first night the auditorium was packed and humming with expectation. Through the show the public remained quite silent. And then, at the end of the show, after its climactic end and blackout, there was a surprising silence. And then, to our complete astonishment, the whole audience stood up and flamencoed their appreciation. The sound of the cries and the stamping was deafening. And it was all thanks to those brave actors and of course to Jane. That night in Seville was an overwhelming experience. So we went on to do several shows at the National and Jane worked on all of them with us. It was a sort of marriage between the three of us ever since.

Lizzie: What did you see in Jane's work that excited you when you first worked with her? What made you want to continue working with Jane?

Declan: Jane came as a choreographer, but actually, that is the least of what Jane does. She does something much, much more than that. What it is is impossible to define, hard even to describe, but she helps to 'locate the actor in the space'. This is not so easy as it sounds, largely because many people don't think there is a problem. Another reason that Jane is extraordinary is because she never seems to get confused. That's fairly unique. Occasionally I feel confused but Jane always seems to see things very clearly and she has tremendous grasp. For myself and Nick she has often shone a light through darkness.

Lizzie: How would you describe what it is that Jane does with the actors to get them into a place where you can work with them?

Declan: Well, we work on it together, but specifically Jane helps to make the actors conscious of their bodies in the space. And, happily, that's also been the centre of our own work. Of course, Jane comes from a different angle, she enters the same artistic space through a different door. But like us she intuits that it is the space that affects us and changes who we are. And she knows how to make that practical. So, it is not that I am 'me in a space'. It's the contrary, it is the space that changes me, the space makes me. No space, then no me. And that is the extraordinary thing that Jane does. She also does unique work to develop what we call 'flow'. She knows how to make these and many things easy to feel and practical to execute. In fact, Jane loathes all pretension. Basically, she sees through any bullshit into what is really happening.

Lizzie: Is there a difference in an actor after Jane has worked with them? Could you describe the difference?

Declan: She's been very good at getting actors out of their heads and away from what I call the tyranny of meaning. And she can release things through movement, quite extraordinary things.

Lizzie: What does Jane's movement work bring to your directing?

Declan: I've learned an enormous amount from Jane over the years just by watching her doing things. For example, she can reassure the actors that the space will look after them. However, Jane's energy is quite different from mine and perhaps that is how she has helped me to direct. If you only classify her as a choreographer, you miss the point. Jane will always remain a towering figure that has changed my life.

Lizzie: How important is it to work with a movement director and why?

Declan: If you are working with text it is crucial that the actors embody that text. They need to get out of their heads and into their bodies. This is really my primary task as a director and a movement director is crucial to this process. The audience has not come just to see a text audibly articulated, or an argument clearly delivered. The audience has come to see experience realised in the bodies of the actors. That is what theatre is and in my view a movement director is central to this process.

Lizzie: How would you describe Jane?

Declan: How would I describe Jane? I wouldn't dare! She's wonderful. She can occasionally be maddening! She is one of our closest friends. We see her regularly and it was sad during lockdown when we couldn't meet. We love her very much. She's very, very, very, very much a 'one off'. How she came to be Jane, well, God knows. A young Spanish friend met her recently and afterwards described her as 'maxima'. Actually, I don't know exactly what is meant by 'maxima', but that's what Jane is, MAXIMA!

Grace Olinski – actor and LAMDA graduate 2020

Grace Olinski is an actor and writer currently based in Brooklyn. She graduated from the BA (Hons) Professional Acting Course at LAMDA in 2020, where she studied with me for three years. I asked Grace to write about her relationship with Pure Movement, both in her training and as a professional actor.

Grace: Actors are often told that their body is their instrument. I agree, I think it's a clear and simple truth. But figuring out exactly what that means and finding a way to play your instrument fully and expressively is a much more nebulous task. I've found that many kinds of movement work will prioritise aesthetic or impressive ability. And yet I've had precious few auditions that came down to whether or not I could do the splits or do a handstand. This work is about something deeper, simpler, and more connected to the actor and their relationship to the world around them.

This work has given me space, weight, connection, and clarity. When I do the work I feel my body gently come alive, and I see the world around me with more curiosity and sensitivity. The relationship between me and my partner, me and the text, me and the space, feels fluid and free. I can stop thinking about what I should do, what something means, how I'm coming across, and simply enjoy where and what I am in that moment.

This work leads me back to the essence of how I exist in my own body. It connects me with that essence, brings it to the surface, and helps me extend and craft it in my work as an actor. It is continuous work, but the foundation is there.

As a teacher, Lizzie strikes the perfect balance of specificity and freedom. Her instructions are clear, insightful and inspiring, but she always leaves space for self-discovery, laying out the stepping stones but letting each person find their own way across. Throughout my training, I looked forward to her classes not only as opportunities to do deep and meaningful work, but as time to stop, breathe and move for the joy of it.

Merry Conway – movement practitioner and actor/creator

This piece of writing is by Merry Conway, movement teacher, creator, performer and film maker, based in the United States. Merry was a mentee of Trish Arnold and continues the long-standing relationship with Kristin Linklater Voice work, regularly travelling to Orkney to train voice teachers. She directed and produced the film entitled *Tea With Trish*. Merry has been instrumental in helping me put this book together in its latter stages. We have spent many hours over Zoom, Merry in New Mexico, US, me in Cambridge, UK, delving deeply into the meaning of the words I have written, in order that they convey a clarity and sincerity that reflects the practice of Pure Movement. I have learnt so much from the hours of conversation with Merry – like Jane, she has helped deepen my understanding of the practice and myself. Here, Merry describes her own journey into Pure Movement.

Merry: I began my lifelong conversation with Trish Arnold's work in the early 1970s. The lineage of this movement work, how it is held by each person, and grown, and passed on, is a beautiful study. Lizzie Ballinger's thoughtful work is a wonderful contribution to that river of practice. Reading her book, I think back to my early days living in London with Jane Gibson as my movement teacher. I took her classes during the early years of her teaching, and I loved her vital work. I particularly took to the swings, as I felt such physical freedom, such pleasure and natural buoyancy. I met Trish Arnold when I subsequently started taking classes at the training programme of Common Stock Theater Company. My enthusiasm for the movement work continued during several years, but it was matched by a need to support myself in London, and

Jane suggested I consider training to be a movement teacher, since I so clearly related to the swing work. Jane guided me and I began as a student teacher at LAMDA, where I followed both her classes and those of Sue Lefton, in the traditional apprenticeship fashion. I still have the notes from every one of those classes, during which I observed one class taught by Jane or Sue, with half the year's students, and then immediately participated in or led the second lot. Conversations and instruction was given to me by both teachers. Trish and I met up when she was free from her busy schedule in both America, Stratford and London. I moved along to my first teaching positions at several Drama Schools in London.

Then, my life trajectory altered and I returned to America; but before I left, Trish and I discussed the possibility of sharing some of her American workload when she could not be there. Thus began a period of closer contact with her, and her generosity and guidance were instrumental in my creative life in America. We divided several years of movement teaching at Carnegie-Mellon University Conservatory programme in the late 1970s – me doing the first half of the year, and she, the second. There was always an overlap when we were together in Pittsburgh, and I gave a good record to her of all the exercises I did, and then she would fill me in on how she continued the work. She guided me into a deeper understanding of how to break down an exercise – she observed intently the students in front of her, and if they were not able to grasp an exercise fully, she would invent intermediary exercises to help them, returning at the end to the larger demand. She taught me about lightness and levity; both in the doing of the work – balancing the gravity release of a swing with the levity of the rebound – but, additionally, in her light touch when giving comments to students. She would offer a suggestion but did not belabour it in a cerebral way, so the student had time and space to meet the comment.

When Kristin Linklater joined Tina Packer creating Shakespeare & Company in Massachussetts in 1978, Kristin wanted Trish to come do movement work, and Trish sent me along to get the ball rolling. For several years thereafter, Trish and I were able to teach together at workshops and for the company there. Her connection with Kristin over many years of work together – at LAMDA, New York University and The Working Theater – informed the work of both of them.

I visited London regularly to see Trish and remained very close with the movement teachers there. Jane and Sue were movement directors and choreographers by then, but when together, we would still invariably get into discussing new thoughts and insights about 'mooooovement'. I remember being at Trish's house one time when Lizzie, then in her Guildhall MA programme, part of the next generation, came to Trish's to discuss her progress.

My creative work focused on performance for many years, and I moved away from teaching. But as Trish got older, I felt a responsibility to do my part to pass along something of her wonderful contributions, and to catch some of who she was as a person, as well as documenting some of her work. The project evolved into *Tea with Trish*, a double DVD, documenting some classes with her, as well as conversations with Trish and commentary from several of the movement teachers in London who had worked with her.

I was so revitalised by Trish, the swings, and the principles of her work, that I started to teach movement again, and I have continued to do so over these past fifteen years. I work primarily with experienced performers or teachers, and many within the Linklater Voice teaching community. In the wide range of movement and performance work that I teach, I always draw on the underlying principles of Trish's movement work. There is no better way to come into relationship with being present, with the risk and the thrill of surrender, than a full body swing. Even in a Clown class, the swing is not a 'warm up exercise', but a whole experience of dropping into gravity, rebounding and being suspended – poised between life and death – in a very Now moment.

Florence Dobson – actor and RADA graduate 2021

———

In this conversation Florence Dobson discusses the joys and frustrations of the work. Originally from the Lake District, Florence graduated from the BA(Hons) in Acting at RADA in 2021. Since, she has worked across film, TV and theatre and has continued her curiosity for movement, Alexander Technique and the journey of discovery through her work.

Florence: When I came here [to RADA], something was able to come out that was blocked for a while. Suddenly having that freedom, not freedom, as the lessons were structured, but having that space to play where you were permitted to get it wrong, it was so hard. And so it was like, what is the idea of getting it wrong? My body would just be so sort of obedient, but then not reaching the moments which actually have breath in them or specificity.

Lizzie: You said the word 'freedom', then you corrected yourself . . . I wonder if it suggests what happens in the very beginning of the training in Pure Movement, this sort of battle between freedom and structure, and then what we learn is that they actually go hand in hand.

Florence: And that you can't really have freedom unless you know what your boundaries are . . . The movement classes would just take you to a completely different place. It felt like it was a vacuum of the day. . . . I loved how we learnt to communicate. . . . Almost like the speech in the class was only to improve the silence, and then the movement that we were creating was to improve the stillness. Stillness has become something that I'm always trying to enjoy. Because I'm so uncomfortable in stillness . . . but when I watch stillness, really be alive, there's nothing more exciting. But there are moments in Pure Movement when the . . . when it's the tiniest movements that hit you the most. I can remember when we'd go from the drops and the swings, then we'd do the sternum work, and there'd be these moments . . . when we'd just be stood, and the sternum would be so fluid that even the slightest tilt down, it was just sudden, a release of something.

I think for me, Pure Movement feels embryonic, it feels like the little seed that the stem, that everything shoots out from . . . I feel like a child that has come from the seed but doesn't quite know . . . but without that seed then . . . the shoots are going in all different directions, it feeds into everything.

And vulnerability, I think Pure Movement hones in on vulnerability, and what vulnerability actually is. Actually going to a place that is totally out of reach, where the movement just feels so . . . yeah . . . it just makes sense, and it doesn't need to make literal sense, but for whatever reason, that needed to come out in that moment, and it makes you in a state of, not readiness, but liveness where anything can happen, and your body can respond before you've even had a chance to say your line . . .

Lizzie: I like that this movement work has allowed you to learn what being vulnerable is in a creative sense, an active sense.

Florence: It's like, honestly, you just don't know how to describe it when it's there . . . it's so overwhelming.

Lizzie: It's just wordless really . . .

Florence: I'd be interested to know from you. . . . why, why we're doing a specific movement . . .? But then you can't know that until it just sits in you. Have you ever done classes where you explain way more about what is going on and why this releases this, for example?

Lizzie: I have notes from Trish Arnold and Jane Gibson where they'd say to me: 'students don't need to know why; they just need to do it'. When I started learning this work at Guildhall I really struggled with that concept, I was the same as you; 'why are we doing this?!' When I first started teaching I didn't really understand why I was doing the movements. But when I came to the mentorship with Jane and I went deeper into the work, I realised that by going through the exploration and the process myself, I was starting to understand the 'why'. I didn't need to ask the questions in the moment and I didn't need to talk about it during the work, I just felt it more in my body.

And I would ask the questions later, Jane and I would discuss the discoveries, but only after I had experienced the work physically, emotionally and sensually. It begins as a visceral experience, and develops into an intellectual one, until the totality of yourself is in full flow, mind and body working together. Not one without the other. It's a thinking movement practice.

The more we all talk about this work during the experience, the less we will discover, it stops you finding things out for yourself. It hinders and interrupts the experience. This is not to say that we can't speak about it after the moment, at the end of a class, and I always encourage this. And I know it's hard to get your head around, it's very hard to trust in a new training, when it's all uncertain. The mentorship and this book is about learning this as a teacher, you have to learn how to hold that space and say it's OK, I know you're all screaming at me internally, I know you're all fighting and resisting and hate me because I'm not giving you what you want right now, but I'm OK with that, I'm going to hold that, and we'll keep going and I'll keep insisting. Knowing that you will get there.

I couldn't do that before the mentorship. I couldn't hold the space, so when I was challenged, when I felt that resistance, I'd make everyone run or play a game and change the energy in the space because it was too intense. . . . so going back to that idea of learning how to be vulnerable, I had to learn to be still, silent and grounded and it be OK; I'm not going to divert attention away, I'm just going to hold it, and it's an exposing place to be, I might blush, I might forget what I'm teaching, but oh, OK, this is alright, we're still in it, we're still discovering things. And in that way it becomes a completely equal relationship in the room.

Florence: And that was one of the powerful things as well, is that you'd be doing it with us, you wouldn't be stood in a corner, instructing us from afar, you'd be in the space with us, and that gives us a sense to trust, because if you're practising what you're preaching, then clearly . . .

Lizzie: And all that comes with that, the tears, the blushing, the falling, the failing, it's all there; I can't ask people to go there if I don't go there myself.

Florence: And when you would come into the space with a clear shift of energy, I'd love how you'd say, 'I'm bringing what I have into the space with me and allowing myself to be changed. . .' I think we're so determined on 'I can't do this because I'm feeling like this right now', and actually you proved all of that wrong because you would come in and it would encourage us to be brave.

The classes were just empowering, it felt like our bodies were able to . . . like a mum needing to let go of the child's hand and just let them fall, you know they're going to fall, the possibility is there, but you just have to let it happen. We got taken to places that our bodies were never permitted to go, or we've never permitted ourselves to go.

If you don't have that trust, how are you going to take risks. Everything is risk really, the suspensions, it's the risk of when the fall is going to happen.

Sue Lefton – Movement Director, theatre director, social and historical dance teacher and choreographer

———

This piece of writing is from Sue Lefton, Movement Director and theatre director with an extensive career working across theatre, opera and film. She is a key inheritor of the movement teaching of Litz Pisk and went on to teach at most of the major drama schools in this country. Sue was Head of Movement at the Guildhall School of Music and Drama for seven years during the 1980s and while studying for my MA taught me historical dance. Sue invited me to assist her on productions such as Rhinoceros at the Royal Court, and to teach some social and historical dance classes at The Guildhall when the occasion arose. I asked Sue to write something about my progress over the years since she had recently observed my teaching Pure Movement at RADA.

Sue: In the late noughties I supervised Lizzie in the field of Social Dance while she was doing an MA in Movement Training for Actors at The Guildhall School of Music and Drama. As an MA student Lizzie took classes alongside younger drama students. I do remember that Lizzie always chose to work discreetly at the very back of the class, but in spite of this, her profound approach to the work and the penetrative power of her presence always drew my eye. At the same time, I occasionally observed Lizzie teach movement to Guildhall students over the two years of her MA. I recall that although she showed serious potential as a movement teacher, she was still clearly a young teacher.

In 2012 Jane Gibson was invited by LAMDA to mentor Lizzie once-a-week for two years. LAMDA's idea was a far sighted one. In my experience it is invaluable for a full-time teacher who is still in their early teaching years, to have the opportunity to be mentored. This enables that teacher to put their learning into immediate practice in their classes. Jane Gibson is well known as a brilliant teacher and Movement Director with a lifetime of experience, and enormous respect in the profession. So, I like to think that Jane and I, who were in our turn influenced by Litz Pisk and Trish Arnold, were by the same token able to pass on our work to Lizzie and that Lizzie will do the same. In this way the 'River of work' will continue to flow.

Jane Gibson and I have been lifetime colleagues. We met first in the 1960s while studying acting at The Central School of Speech and Drama, London, where we were taught movement by the great Litz Pisk. In the 1980s I was invited by Trish Arnold and Jane to teach Social Dance at LAMDA, where Jane had been mentored by Trish. Like Litz Pisk, Trish Arnold was another inspirational movement teacher from whom I learnt much.

Recently I had the opportunity to watch Lizzie teach a Movement class at RADA. Here I saw a mature teacher at work, supremely in control of her subject and her students fully focused. The class had a progression with logic yet fluency towards the final exercise. It was a majestic piece of teaching.

Samuel Tracy – actor and RADA graduate 2021

––––––––––

Samuel Tracy is an actor theatre maker and mover who graduated in 2021 from the BA(Hons) in Acting course at RADA. Born and raised in South West London, Samuel's work ranges from the classical to contemporary.

Samuel: Before I began my training as an actor I had a tendency to compartmentalise the different elements of what it was I considered 'acting' to be. Voice was in one place, the concept of character was in another and movement was off entirely in another direction. It was not until I started connecting with the Pure Movement training and its methodologies that I discovered that there was a fundamental truth – 'movement is everything'. When I first heard this phrase I couldn't wrap my head around it, what did this actually mean? The most important thing about the training is that I had to experience it, through the body in a deeply holistic way. Then as my relationship deepened to the work and I was able to access never before felt sensations and components of the training became connected, I finally understood what that phrase actually meant. If I am alive, truly alive and breathing, I am moving. If I am inside an experience, I am moving. If I am in relation (to something or someone), I am moving. Human behaviour is movement. If something is truly happening to me, I am being moved and affected. If I am truly in communication with someone, I am moving and affecting them. This is a fundamental fact about life, and so therefore a fundamental fact about acting.

As actors we are tasked with being a vessel for communication, for the grand and for the subtle. Usually when a writer or a creator is moved to write or create something there is something important they wish to impart on the world. These things can often be heavy and require one to connect to the weight of the situation. The weight of humanity itself. This isn't always easy and/or safe. For example, my first job outside of training was playing 'Romeo' in *Romeo and Juliet*. Every night without fail I had to come face to face with my own mortality. I had to hear the news of my young wife's death and then be moved to make a choice about how I would deal with that information. To connect with an idea that massive every show (sometimes twice a day) was truly challenging. However, because of the profound internal, spiritual and biochemical shifts that had taken place within me, I understood (in a physical way) how to be in relation to those experiences.

I feel the work now lives inside me in such a subtle yet accessible way that now all I must do to truly connect with it (and this may sound antithetical to everything I have written before) is to stand still. During my classes I would watch Lizzie 'come into stillness' before we'd begin. I would see something completely change in her eyes, infinitesimal but also clearly cosmic shifts were happening on the surface, coming from what seemed like nothing and nowhere. These would present themselves as tears or glimmers, but it was clear something was now different. I didn't understand what was happening in front of me. However, now I understand. It is possible to connect to the true weight of humanity in a single breath. Because I can now do it too. Because even though I may not be moving around dynamically, I can feel my sternum softening, my breath expanding, my weight dropping. I am truly alive. I am truly moving. Ready to move and be moved. Ready to act.

Brad Cook – Movement Director Stratford Festival, Ontario, Canada, movement teacher, actor and mentee

Next is an interview with a movement practitioner called Brad Cook. He is Movement Director and Coach at the Stratford Festival Theatre in Ontario, Canada, a movement teacher, and an actor running his own company. We met when he attended one of my online workshops. I could see immediately that Brad was a very capable movement practitioner with previous experience of this practice. Following a Zoom chat about the teaching and both our journeys into it, we set up some sessions for him to explore the work in more depth, and in particular discover the links between the movement and language. It has developed into a mentorship of sorts, via Zoom; I work from my home in Cambridge and Brad is often in a beautiful theatre space in Ontario. Here we explore how the movements connect to the desire to speak and the impulse behind every thought, every gesture, every moment. Through the movement work I guide and encourage him to find greater risk and a more dynamic and honest relationship to the drop.

Through the tradition of one-to-one teaching I am continuing to pass on the work, and, although the concept of teaching movement via Zoom was once thought of as inconceivable to me pre-pandemic, it is possible to build on the work, to delve deeply and evolve. Brad is prepared to invest in the work and his future, to develop his own practice as a movement practitioner and an actor. I can see the progression in his body and hear it in his conversation as he learns more about himself and Pure Movement, making exciting and thought-provoking discoveries. He is nurturing his own way of passing this on to the actors he works with and the audiences he faces. Even through Zoom.

Lizzie: How did you come across the Pure Movement work?

Brad: I first came across this work eight years ago while working at the Stratford Festival in Ontario, Canada, as an apprentice movement coach. The Stratford Festival has a long history with the Pure Movement work; Trish herself worked there on and off from the 1960s into the 1980s. After my first few sessions I was left feeling equal parts challenged and inspired; I immediately realised why this work is consistently offered as a part of training programmes and I began to see how it could be offered to professional actors as they work their way through demanding and challenging material.

Lizzie: Why have you desired to learn more of the work?

Brad: Having not been introduced to the work in a training programme, I didn't have the opportunity to do it on a daily basis as a student. I find the more I do the work, the more it reveals how it can support the actor and the specific needs of the actor's job. I suppose, at a very simple level, it brings actors back to the fundamentals of their work in an embodied and dynamic approach. It is designed to free the actor's body of unneeded tension, its movements stem from the breath and thought, and if the body and breath are free, the imagination will be, as well. From there the possibilities are truly limitless.

Lizzie: How has Pure Movement shifted your work?

Brad: The introduction of body weight swings has been one of the most enjoyable aspects of what the Pure Movement approach has offered my work as a coach and theatre maker. There is an endless range of combinations of swings that one can play with; the effortless dynamic of the body dropping and suspending, moving from the centre out into space can be applied to any work on character, text or story. A swing can relate to the whole of the human experience; everything you might need to play as an actor can be found in a swing.

Lizzie: How has the work affected the actors you work with?

Brad: Pure Movement offers a way of working through the whole body from the inside out and encourages the actor to reveal themselves through the work. In a spirit of play and creativity, moving from impulse and imagination, actors are invited to bring their whole self to it and discover, in an authentic way, the dynamic nature of their unique body, moving towards transformation.

Lizzie: How have the one-to-one sessions with me shifted your experience and understanding of this practice?

Brad: For nearly a year now, Lizzie and I have met for regular one-on-one sessions over Zoom, a necessary reality and outcome from the Covid 19 pandemic. Doing this work over Zoom is not ideal, but Lizzie has nevertheless found a way to maintain and encourage the depth, nuance and dynamic of the body through the virtual space.

These sessions with Lizzie served as ongoing dates for me to connect, investigate and challenge my understanding of the Pure Movement work.

Some aspects of the work that have continued to shift drastically for me whilst working with Lizzie have been regarding Pure Movement's connection to text and the ability for the work to foster honest spontaneous release, as well as the discovery of sensation and the deep dynamic of impulse. I began the work with an unconscious hold; unknowingly preparing for the experience stopped me from embracing the messiness that can exist in the stories we tell. As this hold began to release, a deeper connection to language and text followed.

Our sessions would often begin discovering sensation through various movements and body weight swings, Lizzie would then offer space for text and play, connecting the dynamic of the movement to the need to connect and speak. Through the work, I feel a shift. Through the work, there is transformation.

What I have enjoyed about our time together is Lizzie's eye for an honest connection in the work, allowing you space to explore and insisting that you never settle for mindless movement.

Her belief in the transformative power of the work is met with her own curiosity, simultaneously holding your feet to the fire and giving space for you to discover what it is for yourself – with nudges, encouragement and occasional corrections, of course.

'Making it your own' is one of the parts of the work that I value the most.

The vocabulary she uses around the work has helped me share the work with students and professionals. Putting my experience of the work into language can be challenging, and through Lizzie's experience and knowledge, she has imparted some poignant words and phrases which can help unlock a door to a new horizon. Lizzie has given us a common language through which to communicate. This book will be an invaluable asset.

Beth Aylesbury – actor and RADA graduate 2022

––––––––

Below is an interview with Beth Alsbury, an actor I trained on the three-year BA(Hons) in Acting course at RADA. Beth is a disabled actor and a wheelchair user. We have travelled on a journey of discovery and adaption that has been eye opening and heartening in the possibilities it has revealed.

When Beth first arrived at RADA they were the only disabled wheelchair user in the year and had very specific needs. The understanding before Beth began their training was that each tutor adapted the teaching to suit Beth in group classes. Alongside this a movement practitioner was employed to offer individual support for Beth throughout the course of their training. For Beth to learn Pure Movement and have the possibility of engaging fully, there needed to be many adaptions. However hard I tried to find these through my own body before the class or during the class, the teaching felt lacking in individual specificity and was not centred around Beth and their individual requirements. The adaptions felt generalised. It was only when I was finally able to have one-to-ones with Beth that we negotiated our way through the movements together and found ways for Beth to work that were tailored specifically for them. We had time and space for both of us to embody the adaptions and experience the sensation of what they were offering the actor's physical instrument. It gave Beth the necessary time to work creatively with their own learning process, to accept limitations and work with them. It also enabled Beth the space to adapt without the pressure of feeling that they had to keep up with the rest of the class. The one-to-ones supported Beth when in a group situation; they were able to use what we had discovered and confidently stay present and follow their own journey.

Beth graduated from RADA in 2022 and has recently performed in *A Christmas Carol* at the RSC.

Beth: It was a culture shock coming from where I'd come from . . .

Lizzie: You came from a background in circus . . .

Beth: And that's all about risk, it was very big and everything was athletic, really creative and you found things but it was very intense, with an end goal in mind. To come into a space where everything was much more subtle, and grounded in a different way, I come from a space where there was no template, Pure Movement had more of a template.

Lizzie: There's structure . . .

Beth: I found it so difficult, I couldn't breathe, I remember so many classes with you just asking me to breathe . . . .

Lizzie: I think that first entry into the world of Pure Movement is really challenging, it's hard for actors to trust that this teaching structure is there to allow creativity, every art form has its technique, everything creative has to start from a place of technique and specificity, otherwise it's expression without any foundation, without any guts.

So that first term was quite intense for you?

Beth: First term we just tried doing it, just me doing the same things as everyone else did, let's just see what happens if you do every single class, just do it, and I did, but I wasn't doing it!

Because I come from such a physical background, I was able to make it look like I was doing the movements, aesthetically, but not really from here. [Points to stomach.]

Lizzie: What you came with was strength, muscularity, an ability to engage through your body, to organise your body, so your journey has been nuanced, I know everyone's is, but to come with all that, there's some big habits there to unravel.

Beth: I was very used to doing my own thing, just getting on with it, and coming here, that was rattling, like I had all this freedom and now I'm being told what to do! Yet nothing was going in, it was going to my head and not filtering through. I think that whole first year lays bare all your insecurities about everything.

Lizzie: You're most likely to pull up your defences, resistances in that first year because you're being shaken, your being asked to go places that are uncomfortable and new.

Is it clear to you now why you were asked to go through that process?

Beth: Oh yes, now I've gone through it, there was definitely a moment where it sinks in, in the second year, like OK, I think when I eventually … once I went along with it, surrendered to it, OK, so stuff is happening, just go with it, and then, oh, stuff is actually happening. Because I'd done that, stuff was accumulating and happening. I was aware of things.

Lizzie: That's a long process isn't it, and that does really take trust, you come into something and you learn to trust, to surrender, that's not something that anyone can expect one to get easily.

Beth: And because I'd come from being so independent, it was so heightened.

Lizzie: To me that's education, and it can be confusing because it feels like one is being told what to do, has to follow some boundaries. But for you to discover that the boundaries and structure were a necessary part of the process, that's a much deeper sort of education than if I let you just be playful and exploratory without any specificity.

Beth: And yes, I would have just done the same things as I always did . . . Because I come from a place that was playful in that sense, I would have just done the same things I'd been doing already, I possibly wouldn't have shifted, it would have taken me much longer. I was definitely lacking in specificity, I had huge, big muscular movements, this athleticism, to show this dynamic thing, and yes of course it has specificity, but its utilitarian specificity.

I move in a different way to everyone else in the class and I need to find and own the specificity, to be able to do the ensemble work. In a way, that is much more accessible because I know the things I need, I have all these building blocks.

Lizzie: It's more choice and therefore you have much more freedom.

Beth: I think I felt like I was being sanitised . . . yeah, but that's because I'd come from a different place. But then going through it, I realised, no, that's completely not what is happening, it was just coming from one extreme into another, and everyone is coming from their own place that makes the light and shadow look a bit different. I'd come from this bright vivid place that made everything look strange to me. Just finding ways to serve my body, I think, was the way in for me, because initially I was just doing it.

Lizzie: I think that was a shift in our training, it became clear that we needed one-to-ones, we needed specific time for us to be able to adapt the work to suit your needs.

Beth: Yes, so I had my own tool kit.

Lizzie: And accepting that your tool kit is different to the rest of the year group at that time.

Beth: Yeah, that they all might do a leg swing that I just don't have an equivalent for, so I just don't do that. And eventually [after the one-to-ones] I get to the point where I am in the class and think 'what does my body need right now' and do that. Initially I would just pause.

Lizzie: But now you think, you explore, you discover, in the moment and adapt. So you have the language to do this now?

Beth: Doing that made me more adept at listening to my body and accessing places I wouldn't have otherwise, for sure, and it also meant when nuanced obstacles came up, I wasn't completely thrown as I already had the tool kit.

Lizzie: And an adaptability. And that's ultimately what we need as actors and artists, an adaptability to go into any situation and be OK, and still be creative and hold on to a structure we have of ourselves and go wherever we're being asked. And each director will ask something different of you, each part, each job.

It's interesting, hearing it now, I know that you resisted in that first year, but it's still hard to hear it as a teacher.

Beth: I just didn't understand, the way my brain works, my neuro-type means I see systems, I see patterns, I predict from patterns. When you're autistic, that's what your brain does. So for me, it can be hard when I'm in an environment where there isn't that map. I can recognise patterns, so once I surrendered more to it, I could see the patterns, and the structures, and then I can use it in a way that works for me. But initially, what the hell is this?! And I had all those habits in the way, and was thinking 'what is this?', but once I was in it . . . it's the initial getting someone in it.

Lizzie: And that's what's hard . . . do we change the beginning to make it a softer entry in?

Beth: No!

Lizzie: Or is it OK to ask that of people and to know that they will fight against it and just trust that you will get there? Because I know that the work works, and you will eventually understand too, that the structure, the technique is necessary for the expression.

Beth: It might be that some people need a road map, they don't need an explanation of what it's for, just a road map. like I do when I get the stool, and the mat, 'we're going to be on the floor, then we'll stand up, then we'll move in the space'... and then I don't think people need more.

We developed a dialogue, once we understood what I needed a bit more, we had a dialogue. And if you're in a space where there is room for ... where your approach is ... where you don't need all the answers, just the idea that I'm struggling with this ... it doesn't necessarily need lots of change.

Lizzie: I don't think it needs lots of words but there does need to be a road map for certain people with particular ways of working, I think it can help everyone.

Beth: I know all the repetitions have purpose, like when you've been doing a swing for ages, but you haven't really been doing a swing you've just been moving your arm around, and then eventually this one time you do it and something actually happens ... and then you're like 'oh my god, that's what that is' and without the repetition ...

Lizzie: and you can't really ever put words into that experience ...

Beth: I think there aren't really any words for a lot of the movements

Lizzie: It's experiential

Beth: Yeah, completely, it's like, just allowing that ... and getting out of your own way, and not being so precious about it, which I think every actor has to go through.

Lizzie: And again, that's part of the education, the process. Surrendering ... letting go of some defences ... I think that's what we're all trying to do in the training.

It's interesting, I have learnt so much from you and how important the dialogue is, especially when the work is so not about dialogue ... you can still bring in moments of conversation that are necessary that won't interrupt the sensations of the work.

Beth: Often, when I have an adaption of a movement, people say 'when I saw you doing that, I realised what the movement was about, because there was another reference point, rather than it being this movement is this movement and this is the only shape it can make ... how else can it be experienced, and it was another reference point for that person. There was a different way to do it . . . it's not just about 'I have to do the movement in this way'.

Because there was a different way of doing it, the dots also connected for me, it isn't about me making the shape.

Lizzie: There is real specificity and the technique does suggest there is a right and wrong. Like in all technique . . .

Beth: The number of conversations we've all had about that; 'they say there is no right and wrong, but clearly there is a right and wrong'.

Lizzie: And there is contradiction in everything we're asking! And certainly, something that goes deep into the body, it is full of contradiction because of our need to understand why we're doing it . . . I was talking about this with Florence, the frustration of 'why don't you just tell us why we're doing it'. And I said 'then you wouldn't discover it for yourself'.

Beth: Yeah, and I think we're all discovering something different.

Lizzie: It comes from you, it's your discovery. And it's a training that speaks to every person in the room. So I set up the structure and the boundaries and this allows you to discover more for yourself.

Beth: No one gets it in first year, but it's like doing your scales, nothing can happen unless you go through that. It's very hard to see that you're building something in your practice. All of us are thinking, 'how is this going to make us a better actor?', no matter how much you think you're not. But you can't know the answer because you don't know what it is yet.

Lizzie: I think it would be sad if we took away all the unknown.

Beth: Especially when you have people with different needs, there are ways of making enough known that makes it functional and keep the unknown. And I think that's what we found, we found the stuff that does need to be known to make it a safe, productive environment, but still kept the unknown. It meant that I didn't need to know everything but knew enough that I could get my head in it and let myself do it and not worry about it all. A lot of people who have different needs from the norm, it's that independence, I need to take care of me. It's a fine line.

Lizzie: It's a balance.

Beth: I think it's about an expansiveness whilst retaining the principles that are necessary to do the work, if we discover there are ones that aren't as flexible as we thought, maybe we can be more flexible with this aspect.

Lizzie: Do you think this practice has adapted for you personally and can continue to be expansive and allow all those questions to come in?

Beth: Yes, if you think back to my first class with you to now, it's completely different, how we approach it is completely different. I think when you're the first person with a different body, I came to the school knowing that mistakes would be made. Everyone was learning around me. And for someone who has different needs from me that will be the same for them, until there have been more bodies through the process it will be a more difficult process for the bodies going through. And that has to be acknowledged I think, otherwise you can't trust. That's why I trusted RADA. . . . Here people admitted they didn't know, and that was brilliant. Honest.

But from our first class to now it has transformed, it has expanded. I can access a class in a way I couldn't before. I could be in the class, before I wasn't 'in it'.

The way you run a class now with me in it is different to how you started with me. We needed the one-to-one support right from the beginning.

When the reference point [in a practice] is made accidentally or is traditionally exclusive, and it wasn't necessarily consciously designed that way but it has been practised in that way, that lays the foundations. [To be expansive and inclusive] you have to work out what principles are flexible and what principles are key, in order for the training to evolve and become accessible to all.

And I think we found that.

Eric Sirikian – actor and RADA graduate 2018

———————

Eric Sirakian trained on the three-year BA(Hons) in Acting course at RADA, graduating in 2018. He has performed in several plays in London, including in the West End and at Shakespeare's Globe, and he made his Broadway debut as Hassan in *The Kite Runner* in 2022.

Eric: The physical work that Lizzie is committed to developing is the foundation for all my work as an actor. I wouldn't dream of stepping on a stage or on a set without waking up my body and engaging my physical imagination. Pure Movement has helped me appreciate that when the body is flexible, open and available, the actor can communicate much more clearly and powerfully. The exercises are precise and exacting, but they also leave lots of room for exploration and play. Lizzie's approach is holistic, integrating breath, voice and text, emphasising impulse and spontaneity, and preparing the actor for work in every kind of role, in every medium. This work is, in short, indispensable. It has given me full command of my craft.

Stephanie Arsoska – movement practitioner and mentee

———————

This next piece of writing is from a movement practitioner, Stephanie Arsoska, who approached me for some individual teaching. We have been working together via Zoom for over a year now as Stephanie is based in Scotland. Stephanie has taught movement-based practices across a range of performing arts courses with a particular interest in improvisation and ensemble theatre practice. She works as a Movement Director and creative mentor to other artists. Having trained as an actor, Stephanie also has a degree in Drama, Applied Theatre and Education from the Royal Central School of Speech and Drama, completed a post-graduate in Physical Theatre Jasmin Vardimond's Dance Company and has an MEd in Teaching and Learning in the Performing Arts from the RCS. Stephanie is an experienced movement practitioner whose curiosity and desire to evolve her own practice has led her to explore Pure Movement and discover how it speaks to her as a teacher and a creator. I asked Stephanie to write down her thoughts about the movement work.

Stephanie: It is challenging to put my experience of the work into words, while it is a very clear and visceral encounter with arriving into my own body, it is also something that feels beyond language.

As a movement teacher to actors in training I have experimented with many approaches to try and support my students on their journey towards connecting with and understanding how to appropriately and efficiently connect with and use their body in performance. I have trained in physical theatre, many movement-based improvisation practices, yoga and Qi Gong, and while all of these different approaches contain useful elements as I taught it became increasingly clear that there was still something missing from what I was offering. The first time I encountered the Pure Movement work through Lizzie I felt that I had found the missing piece that I had been searching for.

The work, for me, is an invitation to come closer to being inside my own body. Often at the start of a session I imagine that I am in a strongly connected place physically but as soon as I start the practice, I discover that I am nowhere near where I thought I was, that there is work to be done to help me really arrive. As I work and I begin to sense and release the weight of my own body, I experience a sense of dropping down, as though falling through trapdoors in the body, I am always surprised by how far it is possible to travel within what appear to be very simple movement tasks. The tasks look simple but are full of possibility and detail. The apparent simplicity of the work allows space for the complexities of the body to fully reveal themselves.

I have experienced my body in a completely new way through this practice. It has been like learning a new language, or rather learning the real language of my body before I layered it over with habits, fears and tension. This is not a practice in which you can hide, in fact I did not even know how much I actually was hiding until the work caught me out over and over again. You cannot pretend to perform in this practice, you will be caught immediately! In this respect the work takes you to a very vulnerable place but I also feel deeply connected to my own potential strength in ways that I have not encountered in other practices.

Ultimately what I find in the work is that I am opening up possibilities in the body. There is an increased spaciousness and a deeper connection to a quality of discovery. I feel very present when I do this work, in a way that allows me to feel prepared to play in a very committed and connected way, which is exactly the quality I am hoping to encourage in the actors I train.

Eduardo Ackerman – actor and LAMDA graduate 2021

————————

Below is an interview with Eduardo Ackerman. Raised in Tijuana, Mexico, and educated in the States, he attended a two-year acting conservatory in France. This was his first introduction to Pure Movement under the guidance of Wendy Allnutt. He then trained with me at LAMDA on the MFA Professional Acting Course, graduating in 2021. During his final year of study, following my departure from LAMDA, he worked privately with me in weekly one-to-ones for a year.

Lizzie: I'm interested in hearing how you work with Pure Movement. How and if your relationship with the work has changed over the course of your training as an actor at LAMDA and then with me.

Eduardo: When I came to LAMDA I was pretty tight, pretty fixed. . . . I was more worried about the technique, and getting it right. I knew that the area of constriction for me was my upper body due to my past athleticism. So I viewed it as 'I need to open up my chest, work more on my upper body, loosen up my hip joints' . . . I was doing Pure Movement to work with the technique. And I think the penny dropped when we started our one-to-ones. As you said, it's not a yoga practice, but I took it as just that, I'm just stretching, I'm just opening. Little did I know the actual profound thing was the expressivity. What you were trying to teach everyone was that this was a discipline, learn it, then you can mess up the rules. Once you know the rules you can mess it up, play with it. And that's where the work actually starts. It's not just about having a loose upper body; it's being absolutely free to follow your own impulses and your own creativity. I could focus on specific characters, bring specific aspects of my characters to you and play with them. All those years that I spent trying to perfect a little technique, I realised . . . no, you can play around with the technique according to the character. You're not caged up with the technique, you can adapt the work so you can tap into the energy [of a character] in a very magical way.

Lizzie: For me, I know the process of the work, how it shifts, flows between technical and expression, and I try to start that relationship early on, but it's difficult for actors to understand that. I know and trust that this does develop over time. It sounds like there was a real progression, a journey there that was necessary for you, that you started with a strong focus on the specificity, and by doing that, it has allowed you to move on to the expression.

Eduardo: The thing I love about any discipline is you have to respect it, to appreciate it, anyone who is hungry and desires something, I think it's imperative to have that discipline, a need to understand . . . for me, once I actually know what I'm doing, and yes, I did take it too far into the technique, but I wouldn't trade that, if it took me two years to get there, I believe those two years will have helped me to grow so much more.

Maybe it's my athletic background, but you see brilliant athletes, you know the way they warm up their bodies, the way they move on the court, the football field, you can see the way they juggle the ball, they have this effortlessness, because it's been years of playing around with the ball, but for me acting is the same. A director told me once that they can spot the experienced actors because the first thing they do is to walk around the stage and take in the space, before anything else. For me that's the technique, it's those little things that really matter, and that's what I would like to do. Yes, you brought it in to the teaching early on, the balance of technique and expression, but for me I had to take my time with it. I had to go too far to come through it and realise it's all about the expression coming out of the technique.

Lizzie: I've been asked how this work is adapting with the big changes going on in training.

Eduardo: Is the work valuable? If it is it will uphold any movement. It will adapt with the changes. I just loved the practice from the word go.

Lizzie: You had a physical training already, and that helped, you've come from a place where you are used to being pushed quite hard, a discipline, but not everyone comes with that work ethic. And that's where the boundaries in the work help. For people who haven't come from that background, by holding the boundaries it gives people something to press against, they then realise for themselves, they understand what the space is doing, or allowing, and how it helps them, not me, helps them to slow down, provides them a safe space to explore and be creative.

Eduardo: I remember after 6 months of doing Pure Movement I went home for Christmas and went to a party, I realised that people were treating me differently and I couldn't understand why. Then I worked it out, I was taking my space, owning the space, that's what I'd been doing in the training and it was now affecting things in my life. In a positive way. And I really believe that Pure Movement gave me that attunement, that awareness.

Lizzie: In my mentorship, through the work it brought me much more into myself, I found that I could take the space unapologetically, there is something about coming into yourself and gaining your strength. I think that's where the value of the work goes deeper, because it will stay with you even if you don't go into acting. Yes, it gives you expression, dynamic, loosens the body, but it also allows you to connect a little bit more to your spirit and that's the bit that moves me. And I think it moves a lot of people but it's hard to articulate it, or even notice sometimes.

I wonder how it connects to your acting; some people say it's hard to make the connections during the training.

Eduardo: That's a question that a lot of people ask … It is so hard to explain, I can't understand why it's so hard, I can feel it, in a scene, I don't even think about it, I just know I have the freedom to do something because of the Pure Movement training. In the past 6 months the thing people have picked up on the most is the movement in my acting, in a scene, in every project, and I'm not focusing on movement in particular … so the answer is very obvious, I just did the work. . . . I do it over and over again until I forget about it.

The thing that sticks for me is the duality, you always talk about this, the opposing argument, heaven and hell, going forwards or backwards, the opposition. Once my body understands that potential, I'm just aware of it, doing all those movements, it helps me to understand this in all the texts I work with, the opposites that exist, the other pull. My body understands it in a physical way and that's helped me to understand it in an intellectual way.

Shakespeare, for example, it used to daunt me. My speech patterns would be so staccato, I would bring the speech down to me, I wasn't able to match the rhythm of the character or the language, as soon as I worked with movement . . . I realised how much more free I was to change quickly in-between thoughts. I could find new colours, find the thoughts in the moment. And it was working with the challenging texts that really allowed me to see how much the movement work had helped me. Had shifted me.

Lizzie: It's great to hear because I know why the work can help an actor find all those things in language, in the text, but it's great to hear you have discovered it. There's complexity in the work, it's a thinking practice, it's not just about sensation, it's putting everything together, the mind and the body.

Eduardo: It's essential for any actor, I feel it, I know it, but you have to dig, you have to keep digging . . .

Lizzie: And it doesn't ever really stop.

Daniel Bowerbank – mentee, actor and RADA graduate 2020

———

Daniel Bowerbank is an actor and a trainee movement practitioner currently being mentored by me through a RADA scheme. He graduated from the three-year actor training at RADA in 2020. As an acting student it was clear he had an instinct for this movement work, and as his training progressed he shifted away from the habitual patterns of his musical theatre background and found an honest relationship with his expressive and dynamic physicality in support of his acting.

Daniel is a young, black actor from Jamaican and Barbadian descent. It is important to me that this practice becomes more diverse in its teachers, that I take active steps towards diversifying this 'River of Movement' as Trish called it. And that those students from Black and Global Majority backgrounds see movement tutors that reflect the rich diversity of our society.

For his mentorship Daniel has weekly one-to-ones with me, when busy schedules allow, and is participating in a movement class and observing the next – a blended mentorship from my experiences at Guildhall and with Jane Gibson. It is a joy to see him discovering the movement work on a deeper level, learning how to hold the space and lead a class. I offered him some questions about his journey with Pure Movement.

Lizzie: What was your relationship with Pure Movement whilst you were training at RADA as an actor? How did the work affect you/move you?

Daniel: I have always loved this work, and really appreciated the classes while training especially for its desire to allow the body to move towards a state of truthful, honest and sincere communication, almost transparent, where the inward state of the actor could be expressed through the body – by way of breath, one's relationship with one's own weight and the body's relationship to space, but also for the understanding that one's physical expression is as important in its stillness as in its movement, and no less expressive.

Lizzie: What has been different about coming into RADA as a trainee teacher of Pure Movement and participating/observing? How are you now seeing the work?

Daniel: One of the major differences has been the perspective shift, from being a student participating in the work, to now being an observer viewing the class from a whole new lens. The body really does communicate and how powerful it is as an observer to see the students connecting at depth with very subtle movements – whether it be letting the full weight of their head drop, or their sternum sink and release; shifting them emotionally, physically and deepening their work as actors, and also to witness people being so free and moving with such abandon has been breath-taking to witness. I must confess, I've shed a few tears watching. But more importantly, I have really noticed, and come to understand that the freedom and courage of these actors in the room, would not be possible without the space in which you create being held in such a way that facilitates breath-taking work.

Lizzie: How do you feel this movement practice relates to the work you continue to do as an actor?

Daniel: This work provides me with an understanding of how much the body speaks and the wealth of stories that are communicated before we even open our mouths. That knowledge has been really invaluable in liberating myself, but this work has also encouraged such bravery in its demand and call for honesty, sincerity and a total relinquishing; to allow oneself to be changed and to truly discover moment to moment through the movement of the body. The freedom I feel when participating in this work is also something I want to share with young people from all backgrounds, who may not have access to the work, to allow them to feel the power that this practice provides and how you can and deserve to take up space, and to come in contact truly with the feelings, emotions and stories that the body holds.

Lizzie: You are a young actor of Jamaican and Bajan decent, now training to be a movement teacher, how does this speak to you?

Daniel: Growing up immersed in West Indian culture, there is such a rich language of the body and its relationship with story, music, words and spirituality; learning more and taking part in this movement practice over the years has unearthed many connections and parallels to my own culture, and others of the African Diaspora. I have always been interested in the body in space and as a vehicle to tell stories, but also the legacy of the body's relationship with the drum and what is conjured within our bodies on an ancestral level when we permit ourselves to yield to its sound. And the importance and significance of drums symbolically – in rituals and ceremonies in many communities across the globe and throughout history, and how that work, discovery and knowledge observed can be infused into my practice as a movement teacher, in the hopes of continuing to enrich and unearth greater depths in the Pure Movement work.

Lewis Merrylees – acting student RADA

———

Lewis Merrylees is from Glasgow, Scotland, and is currently intermitting his studies at RADA. In August 2021 he developed Covid 19, which unfortunately developed into a long-term illness, Long Covid. This forced him to take time away from RADA and seventeen months on he is still experiencing after-effects. Lewis is planning to return to RADA and continue his training. Before his illness, I asked him to record some thoughts about his Pure Movement training.

Lewis: Thoughts about movement ... we were talking about how it's my favourite class. I was so afraid, as Lewis, as me, to do anything that would be uncharacteristic, push the line. I feel like in movement, I'm no longer Lewis, you're just kind of things in a room, like vibrations in the space, you just kind of 'do', and the only limits you put on yourself are yours and yours only.

I suppose I've learnt since then that out of the movement room it's the exact same thing. It's just a beautiful space. It's the space where I leave the classroom and I feel indestructible, I feel like someone could ask me to be in any scene of any play, anything, a film, a pantomime, a podcast, whatever it is and I could do it, I could do it unapologetically, with power, with gravitas, without inhibition, that is it. My gosh, that's it. Pure Movement with Lizzie should be renamed, 'Free your Inhibition' ... is that not a song? There you go, cliches for a reason.

You don't ever have time to question yourself. You may start with something very simple and you end up... I always think if I looked at myself forty minutes into the class and you said, go do that, I'd say no way. But the build-up of it slowly pushes your boundaries, slowly pushes your limits and you start to do stuff without even thinking or realising you're doing it and you finish the class and you think, if I'm capable of that, what else am I capable of?

It's also a beautiful way of experiencing other human beings. In day-to-day life, you never get to experience other human beings on this level. ... you connect over the sheer human form. You can share a moment with someone that is so abnormally normal, so unapologetic.

To discover your own power is something crazy, isn't it? When you discover you can be whatever you want to be. And it's all transferable. It's where I feel the freest and have the most fun. Thank you, Lizzie!

Olivia Nakintu – actor and LAMDA graduate 2021

───────

Olivia Nakintu is a British actor who graduated from the three-year BA(Hons) Professional Acting course at LAMDA in 2020. She is known for her onscreen roles in *Better* (2023), *Am I Being Unreasonable?* (2022) and *Vera* (2011).

Olivia: Undertaking Lizzie's Pure Movement work during my time at LAMDA completely transformed my relationship with my body, as well as my physical approach to acting. Her work has opened up my body in a way that enables it to play and explore in a way that it never has before.

In the early stages, this work may seem so unconventional and challenging that you may resist it – as I tried to myself – but be patient and trust it. Risk, play and dare to enjoy the discomfort of being in the unknown and looking a bit silly! It will only serve you in the long run and aid you in producing a more specific and refined performance. This stuff is gold dust!

Melanie Joyce Bermudez – final year acting student, RADA

───────

Melanie Joyce Bermudez is in her final year of training on the BA(Hons) in Acting course at RADA. Growing up in London from a low socioeconomic background, she had no connection to the arts but found her way into youth companies such as the Lyric Hammersmith, High Rise Theatre and the Open Door Programme before securing her place at RADA. During her training she was attending the Royal Court and Soho Writers Group. I asked Melanie to write about her relationship with Pure Movement.

Melanie: I always believed myself to lead cerebrally. I realise now that this was a protective instinct based on my relationship with academia, the education system and fear. My tendency to seek understanding of things, get them right, and feel, look and show that I may know what I am doing came crumbling in Pure Movement in my first year at RADA. The artificiality and disconnect from desiring in order to 'just get by unnoticed' was exposing. The focus on 'getting it right' became at odds with the movement training which meant it became at odds with my immediate comfortability. My idea of movement had been skewed by a lot of what I thought looked nice, as opposed to moving that is meant.

The encouragement of breath was one of many things that helped me move away from the presentational approach. It enabled each exercise to respire and affect me. Gone were the days where I felt detached from a swing or a drop (this, of course, is always a work in progress). Stepping into my power made me feel vulnerable and alive. Pure Movement demanded of me the physical embodiment of space by encouraging me to be in relationship with it. It made me feel twice my size because my need was five times my size, it was beyond me and it was mine for the taking, even if its manifestation was in the slight turn of a palm or a huge gallop across the room. When I had the courage to connect to this and offer my body to that want, the body told the story. All of the voices in my head that put me in doubt were obliterated by the sensation of need or loss or grief or whatever the text required.

Naturally, it is easy at first to compartmentalise departments when training. The day I dared to truly allow them all to work in tandem was by virtue of Lizzie's work, giving us permission to emulsify with text and with one another at the end of her classes. In spite of us being individuals, we felt at one with one another by not denying the existence of our energies, unafraid to interact, affect and be affected. I credit this safe space and opportunity to how wonderful my year group have become as an ensemble. The introduction of text from our respective projects and using the tools we had just explored in the space through play is truly the foundation of my acting.

Pure Movement has empowered me to feel enough courage to accept my body as a free thinking, responsive and deserving vehicle for storytelling; capable of responding to an offer with honesty, conviction, detail and with absolute purpose, and in service of the story. Each of the exercises we have done have been practised to a meticulous specificity, and (with practice and consistency, of course), now in my third year, I am on the surface of achieving an intimate relationship with my physical language that has ease and efficiency. Pre-training it was impossible to imagine our bodies in the space like a musician and their instrument, knowing the fundamental scales intimately in order to explore and play with the multiplicity of opportunity, choice and possibility within that framework, and yet it makes so much sense. Once you have cultivated a relationship with this work, it is hard, if not impossible, to not stare into the face of your body's potential when you yourself have repeated movements, each of which tell and have told a thousand stories.

None of this would be nearly possible had it not come from a tutor with such sensitivity and unyielding discipline; with an ability to sense the collective and individual pulse of a room and make them feel safe enough to let go and, in turn, trust one another. The amount of trust we all have in Lizzie is because her dedication, compassion and openness to be vulnerable with us is palpable, respected and admired. I am absolute in stressing that Lizzie's Pure Movement work is life-changing, both in the world of acting and in my own life. There have been many things in my life that have signalled danger and alarm, fear and distrust, anxiety and fear which have made me avoidant and ashamed. I have, however, never felt safer and simultaneously more challenged and supported like this in all my years. Pure Movement and Lizzie have taught me so much that I know I have not yet and perhaps never will be able to verbally articulate, but I know my body will.

Francis Lovehall – actor and RADA graduate 2019

Francis Lovehall graduated from the three-year BA(Hons) Acting course at RADA in 2019. He made his stage debut at The Bridge Theatre in Nick Hytner's A Midsummer Night's Dream and has (at the time of writing) been nominated for The Evening Standard Theatre Award for Emerging Talent for his leading role in Red Pitch at the Bush Theatre. Film and TV include Steve McQueen's Small Axe: Lovers Rock and BBC/HBO's His Dark Materials. Upcoming credits include productions for Apple TV and BBC/Netflix.

Francis: My assumption was acting and moving were very different and separate things. The training enabled me to bridge that gap. As stupid as it sounds, I never thought about movement when acting came to mind. until I wanted to be different, other than myself. But mostly feel other than myself.

The epiphany was during a 'Lizzie movement class'. I was struggling to correlate how I could use movement to help with the American realism project we were doing at the time. I felt stuck. Like everything I was doing was coming from the same place physically. My 'natural form' was taking away from the characters form. Not only was I frustrated, I was unaware of what I was physically doing that kept blocking me.

Then Lizzie says to me:

'Breathe in the space with your eyes and your heart'.

This never left me. It taught me that life only flows through clear open spaces. And that's what movement and breath creates for us. Even on the most stressful days on set, or week 3 of rehearsals, with little time and everything spinning. Remember to stop, breathe, and think . . .

'Am I open to everything around me?'

————

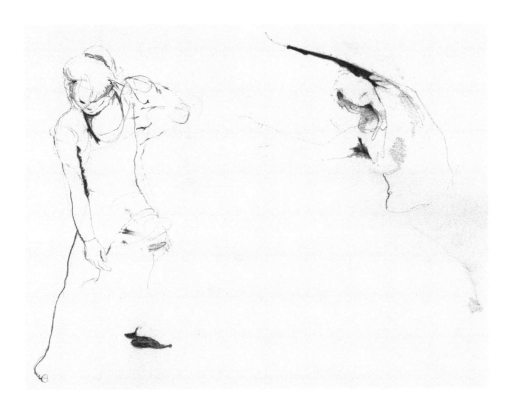

Conclusion

I think this [movement] can be one of the hardest parts of training to become an actor because it is difficult to accept that one's own body is inadequate to achieve this. Musicians, dancers, singers and painters do not have this problem because they must first achieve a specific level of technical ability before they can progress to their full potential. Acting is an amorphous art and TV gives the young aspirant the idea that if one is 'natural' that is all that is needed. Actually no acting is natural.

I believe that the actor has to give up some of the habits they have accumulated. This means taking risks and that can be frightening, i.e. they have always stood with a displaced spine, a collapsed chest and poking neck, locked knees, drooping shoulders etc. etc. (not necessarily the whole catalogue!). It is hard to change because habitual attitudes are safe. But they must unlock their expressive, imaginative body.

Trish Arnold

Those who explore the depths of this practice have an embodied understanding that the work works. This comes from a commitment to the impulsive and dynamic physical instrument, the body, as the foundation to all acting. It reveals the individual's physical expression. By exploring a natural and organic relationship with gravity and levity through swings and stretches, an actor discovers clarity of intention, a fullness in how they organise their body creatively in space. And a freedom to play emerges – the actor is then in a space where they can truly create theatre. Jane Gibson once said that her body only really shifted when she worked with Trish Arnold; she had previously been taught by Litz Pisk and Jacques Lecoq, both esteemed, dynamic movement teachers who incorporated weight and the swing into their practice, but Jane credited the detailed teaching of Trish Arnold with transforming her body into an instrument of expression.

Slow down, it's not a performance, the dramatic possibilities come by themselves, no need to rush for it.

Jane Gibson

I have worked with many actors during their training and it never ceases to amaze me how every single body shifts, transforms and grows in strength, openness, availability and expressivity. It is a practice that honours the individual, the artist, whatever they bring with them, whatever their background, with whatever perceived limitations they carry with them. It challenges them, changes them. It moves them. And from this point onwards they are free to move their audience.

It isn't a system; the movements have an openness and fluidity, like the world we live in.

Jane Gibson

Engage with the many movements for yourself, practise them with commitment and openness, play with a spirit of discovery and decide for yourself what defines Trish Arnold's practice. Breathe through them, allow yourself to be moved by the sensations you experience, insist on working with precision, a specificity that Trish believed was absolutely necessary for corporal sincerity and clarity of expression. Connect deeply into your spine, let it awaken your spirit, and hopefully you will experience the uniqueness in the work. And it only works when it is owned, embodied and passed on through the act of moving and being moved.

References

Listed in order of appearance

Jane Gibson: Movement Director and Choreographer. Gibson trained as an actress at Central School of Speech and Drama and with Ecole Jacques Lecoq in Paris with Philippe Gaulier. She was a student teacher under Trish Arnold at LAMDA and worked in professional theatre and actor training for several years. Gibson was Head of Movement at the National Theatre for ten years under Richard Eyre and is Associate Director of Cheek By Jowl. She has worked extensively as a movement director and choreographer for the RSC, the National Theatre and the Royal Opera House, amongst others.

Michel Saint-Denis: (1897–1971) Actor, writer, director and teacher, Saint-Denis's philosophies greatly influenced twentieth-century European theatre. Nephew of Jacques Copeau, Saint-Denis worked with his uncle's company, Théâtre du Vieux-Colombier, for several years before moving to London and setting up the London Theatre Studio in 1935, an actor training based on the principles of Copeau and his own developing practices. In 1947 Saint-Denis founded the Old Vic School which provided actor training until 1952. He went on to direct and teach at many establishments across the globe, including the Julliard Drama School and the National School of Theatre, Canada.

Meyerhold: (1874–1940) Russian director, actor and practitioner, developed an actor training known as biomechanics, where learnt physical gestures and movements expressed emotional states. Meyerhold began his career learning from Stanislavsky. He moved away from Stanislavsky's naturalistic teaching to form his own more stylised theatre, influenced by traditions such as Commedia dell'arte.

Litz Pisk: (1909–1997) Austrian Movement Director and practitioner who revolutionised actor movement training in twentieth-century Britain. She began her career in Vienna working as a movement teacher and a designer, having a gift for both. After moving to England in the 1930s, Pisk taught movement at RADA and joined Michel Saint-Denis at the short-lived Old Vic Theatre School. Her close collaboration with director Michael Elliot placed her as one of the country's most notable Movement Directors and she continued to work in theatre and actor training, including six years as Head of Movement at Central School of Speech and Drama, until her retirement in 1970.

Edward Gordon Craig: (1872–1966) Craig was a radical and influential theatre director and designer of international theatre in the twentieth century as well as a prolific writer. Born in England, he began his career as an actor but soon moved into design for productions and directing. He founded the

School for the Art of the Theatre in Italy in 1903, a training in theatrical design, and directed and designed performances for Stanislavsky at the Moscow Art Theatre. As a writer he published journals and several books, including *Towards a New Theatre*. His innovations include the use of mobile screens or flats to be used as a staging device and moving away from footlights to lighting from above.

Jacques Lecoq: (1921–1999) At the beginning of his career, Lecoq studied sport and physical education. In 1945 he joined an acting company with Jean Dasté called the *Comédiens de Grenoble*. Here he discovered Copeau's philosophies and ran the company's physical training. From 1948–1956 Lecoq lived and worked in Italy, directing productions and developing his mask work with the sculptor Amleto Sartori. Returning to Paris in 1956, Lecoq opened his School of Mime and Theatre while also teaching at the Ecole Nationale Supérieure des Beaux-Arts. He developed a 'teaching programme on architecture based on the human body, movement and the "dynamics of mime".'[1] Lecoq's wife, Fay Lees Lecoq, continued his work running the school after his death and it continues to be a training establishment today under the leadership of their daughter, Pascale Lecoq.

Sigurd Leeder: (1902–1981) A German dancer, choreographer and teacher, Leeder was born in Hamburg. He studied dance under Sarah Norden and joined several dance companies in Germany during the early 1920s. In 1924 he met Kurt Jooss whilst dancing at the Stadttheater in Münster, the beginning of a long collaboration that lasted twenty-three years. In 1934 Leeder and Jooss came to England and formed the Jooss-Leeder Dance Studio at Dartington Hall in Devon. Leeder departed from Jooss in 1946 and set up his own studio in London. Until his death in 1981, he continued to teach in London and internationally, including directing the University of Chile's dance department from 1959 to 1964.

Kurt Jooss: (1901–1979) Jooss, a dancer, choreographer and teacher, born in Germany and best known for his revolutionary style of dance that combined classical ballet with modern dance and theatre. After meeting and working with Rudolf Laban, Jooss set up his own company called *Die Neue Tanzbühne*. Here he joined forces with the composer Fritz Cohen, with whom he continued to work for many years. He collaborated with Sigurd Leeder and together they created Joss's most famous piece entitled *The Green Table*, in 1932. After fleeing Nazi Germany Jooss and Leeder set up a training programme at Dartington Hall, Devon. Jooss returned to Eessen, Germany, in 1949 and continued to teach and choreograph.

Michael MacOwan: (1906–1980) MacOwan was a director and teacher of acting who had worked with Michel Saint-Denis at the Old Vic Theatre School, London. He set up the experimental London Mask Company and became Principal of LAMDA in 1958 and remained so until 1966.

Norman Ayrton: (1924–2017) Born in London, Ayrton was an actor, director and teacher. He trained at the Old Vic School under Michel Saint-Denis and joined the company for one year where his focus was on movement for the actors. In 1952 Ayrton set up his own Studio in London and began coaching at the Royal Opera House. He later joined the faculty at LAMDA where he was Head of Movement before becoming Principal in 1966 following MacOwan's retirement from the post.

---

[1]http://www.ecole-jacqueslecoq.com/school-history/?lang=en

Iris Warren: Voice teacher, Warren had her own private studio In London and taught at the London Theatre Studio and at the Old Vic Theatre School with Michel Saint-Denis in the late 1940s/early 1950s. She joined LAMDA in the 1950s and is responsible for creating a new actor training in Britain alongside Michael MacOwan and Norman Ayrton. Warren's voice philosophies revolutionised vocal training in its relationship between emotional release and the voice. Tutored Kristin Linklater when she joined the LAMDA faculty in 1958.

Merry Conway: A movement practitioner, teacher, creator and one of Trish Arnold's mentees who uses the movement work alongside her own practice in America. Born in New Mexico, US, trained at LAMDA, Conway continues the longstanding collaboration with the Kristin Linklater Voice Centre. She produced and directed the film entitled *Tea With Trish,* in 2009; a fascinating visual documentation of Trish Arnold, accompanied by conversations with the many UK-based movement teachers who have found themselves drawn to Trish Arnold's work.

London Theatre Studio: A training school for drama and design students founded by Michel Saint-Denis in 1935, in Islington, London. 'The name Studio was deliberately chosen and the intention was that a company would be formed and fed by students, designers, directors and technicians from the Studio, but also that professional actors would be able to take classes to refresh or extend their skills.' The school closed at the beginning of the Second World War in 1939.[2]

Old Vic School: Opened in 1947 as a training school and company for actors in the bombed site of the Old Vic Theatre in Waterloo, London. It was formed by Michel Saint-Denis, Glen Byam Shaw and George Devine and closed due to lack of funding in 1952. Its tutors included Michael MacOwan, Norman Ayrton, Litz Pisk and Iris Warren.

Celia Gore Booth: (1946–1992) A British actress born in London who studied acting at LAMDA for three years. Following this she trained in Paris with Jacques Lecoq and co-founded the dynamic company Shared Experience with Mike Alfreds on her return to London in 1975. She had an extensive career as an actress in theatre, film and TV.

Wendy Allnutt: Allnutt is an actress and movement teacher. She studied acting at Central school of Speech and Drama and had an extensive career in theatre, film and TV. She joined Guildhall School of Music and Drama in the 1990s under Trish Arnold and held the position of Head of Movement at the school from 1996 to 2015. She has worked as a Movement Director and movement teacher in many productions and many schools in the UK and internationally.

Sue Lefton: Lefton is a Movement Director and theatre director with an extensive career working across theatre, opera and film. She is a key inheritor of the movement teaching of Litz Pisk and went on to teach at most of the major drama schools in this country. Lefton was Head of Movement at the Guildhall School of Music and Drama for seven years during the 1980s.

---

[2]https://michelsaintdenis.net/the-london-theatre-studio-by-sophie-jump/

Shona Morris: Morris is an actor, movement teacher and Movement Director. She trained at the Ecole Jacques Lecoq and has worked with Trish Arnold. Morris was Head of Acting and Movement at Drama Centre, London, before leading the movement department at RADA for seven years, leaving the post in 2022.

Jackie Snow: Snow is a movement teacher and Movement Director. She trained as a teacher and dancer at the London College of Dance and Drama. She taught at Guildhall School of Music and Drama where she worked with Trish Arnold and has been Head of Movement at RADA and MMU. Snow has worked professionally as a Movement Director in theatre and film.

Susan Dibble: Dibble is a movement teacher, dancer, choreographer and painter based in the US. She trained with Trish Arnold and is a close colleague and collaborator of Merry Conway. Dibble is Director of Movement and Dance Training, Resident Choreographer and Master Teacher for Shakespeare & Company in Lenox, MA. She is on the faculty at Brandeis University and is Director of Dibble Dance Theater, her own performance company that has run for forty years.

Kirstin Wold: Actor, director, choreographer and teacher based in Massachusetts, US. She has directed numerous productions for Connecticut Repertory Theatre and has an extensive acting resume. Wold teaches acting and movement for the actor at Connecticut University and has been a member of Shakespeare & Company in Lenox, MA, since 1987 where she also teaches text and movement.

Kristin Linklater: (1936–2020) A voice and acting teacher and author, Linklater was born in Orkney, Scotland, and trained as an actor at LAMDA where she met Iris Warren. She trained as a voice teacher under Warren and taught at LAMDA alongside Trish Arnold for six years. She opened her own private studio in New York in 1963, and taught at New York University Graduate Theatre Program and Shakespeare Festival, Stratford, Ontario, amongst others. In 1978 she co-founded Shakespeare & Company with Tina Packer and set up her teacher training centre in Orkney, Scotland, in 2014. Linklater has written several voice books including *Freeing the Natural Voice*, 1976.

William Gaskell: (1930–2016) Gaskill was an English theatre director, born in Shipley, Yorkshire, UK. Having studied at Oxford University where he began directing, he went on run the Royal Court, directed numerous productions for the National Theatre and was Artistic Director of the English Stage Company at the Royal Court between 1965 and 1972. He co-founded Joint Stock Theatre Company.

Peter Gill: Gill is a Welsh theatre director, playwright and actor. He began his career as an actor in theatre, film and TV. In 1964 Gill had turned to directing and became Assistant Director at the Royal Court Theatre, later to become Associate Director. He was Artistic Director of the Riverside Studios and Associate Director of the National Theatre where he founded the National Theatre Studio.

Michael Langham: (1919–2011) Langham was an actor and theatre director who built his reputation directing at the Old Vic and Stratford-upon-Avon. Other credits include the National Theatre. His work moved to Canada and he became Artistic Director for the Stratford Festival theatre in Ontario where he redesigned the Stratford Festival's thrust stage in 1962. He joined the Guthrie theatre in Minneapolis. He was director of the Juilliard School's drama division in New York from 1979 to 1992.

Peter Kass: (1923–2008) Kass was an American actor and theatre director who went on to become a prominent teacher of acting. He set up The Working Theatre with Kristin Linklater in 1963, a private studio training actors.

Joe Chaikin: (1935–2003) An American actor and director, Chaikin was a key player in the New York experimental theatre movement of the 1960s. He set up the Open Theatre collective in New York and was a close collaborator of the playwright Sam Shepard. He worked as a director and teacher across the globe, including the Royal Shakespeare Company, the Royal Court Theatre, and ran the Working Theatre with Kristin Linklater and Peter Kass.

Shakespeare & Company: A professional theatre company in Lenox, MA founded by Tina Packer and Kristin Linklater. The company perform a range of plays and provide actor training, incorporating voice and movement.

Frank Whitten: (1942–2011) Born in New Zealand, Whitten was a teacher of drama and a leading actor in theatre, film and TV. He trained as an actor at LAMDA, continued to teach following his graduation and became Vice-Principal in 1970. Following his resignation from LAMDA he founded Common Stock, an Arts Council-funded company dedicated to community theatre along with Chattie Salaman. In 1982 Whitten returned to New Zealand and continued to act with numerous roles in film and theatre.

Chattie Salaman: (1919–2000) Salaman was an English Actress with an extensive career in theatre, film and TV. She also taught and directed in actor training, Guildhall School of Music and Drama amongst others. She was married to John Blatchley who founded the Drama Centre, London and co-founded Common Stock with Frank Whitten.

Tina Packer: Born in England, UK, Packer trained at RADA and worked extensively as an actor in the West End, TV and film. She was an associate artist at the RSC. In 1978 Packer founded Shakespeare & Company, in Lenox, MA, with Kristin Linklater, and stepped down from being Artistic Director of the company in 2009. She is also a writer and teacher.

Karen Beaumont: An actor, teacher and director, Beaumont trained at the Canadian Mime School, Lecoq School of Paris with Philippe Gaulier and with Trish Arnold at Guildhall School of Music and Drama. She became a core member of Shakespeare & Company in 1983 and has an extensive resume of directing and teaching in the US.

Patsy Rodenburg OBE: Rodenburg is a British voice coach, theatre director and author. She was Head of Voice at Guildhall School of Speech and Drama and has worked with the RSC and the National Theatre. She trained in voice studies at Central School of Speech and Drama and worked as an actress before turning to voice work. Rodenburg was Director of Voice at Michael Howard Studios in New York from 1982 to 2020, and in 2015 set up the Patsy Rodenburg Centre for Voice and Speech in New York. She has written several books on the voice including *The Right to Speak* (1993) and *The Actor Speaks* (2002).

Jan Doet: (1909–1988) Doat was a French actor, writer, teacher and theatre director. He published several short books on theatre practices, including *L'expression corporelle du Comédien* (1942) and *Architecture et décors de théâtre* (1931). He was invited to become the director of the Quebec Theatre School, Canada, and taught at the Laval University in Quebec.

Jacques Copeau: (1879–1949) Copeau was a French theatre director, actor, theatre critic and teacher who set up the Theatre du Vieux-Colombier in Paris in 1913. Copeau revolutionised French theatre by concentrating on training actors with high emphasis on the body and voice. He is seen as one of the greatest twentieth-century dramatists and influenced many including his nephew, Michel Saint-Denis.

Sir Richard Eyre CH CBE: Born 1943 in Devon, England, Eyre is a film, theatre, television and opera director. Educated at Cambridge University, he was Artistic Director of the National Theatre between 1987 and 1997. With an extensive résumé Eyre has won several awards including an Olivier Lifetime Achievement Award.

Declan Donnellan OBE: Donnellan is joint Artistic Director of Cheek By Jowl with his partner and designer, Nic Ormerod OBE. The company was founded in 1981 and has performed all over the world. Donnellan, who was born in England to Irish parents and studied at Cambridge University, also directed a feature film, *Bel Ami* in 2012, and writer of *The Actor and his Target* (2005), originally published in Russian in 1999. The company has won numerous awards. Jane Gibson is an associate director of the company and has worked with Cheek By Jowl for over thirty years.

Daniel McGrath: McGrath is an actor, movement teacher and movement director. He trained as an actor at Guildhall School of Music and Drama and subsequently with Phillippe Gaulier. He was Head of Movement at GSMD from 2015 to 2020 and his movement practice has been influenced by Trish Arnold, Wendy Allnutt, Shona Morris and Sue Lefton. He has worked professionally in theatre and TV as a Movement Director.

Bibliography

Listed in alphabetical order

Arbeau, Thoinot. *Orchesography*. New York: Dover Publications Inc, 1967.

Braun, Edward. *Meyerhold on Theatre*. London: Methuen, 1969.

Cameron, Julia. *The Artist's Way: A Course in Discovering and Recovering your Creative Self*. London: Pan Books, 1995.

Chekhov, Michael. *To the Actor on the Technique of Acting*. London: Routledge, 2002.

Cowell, Philip and Hilderbrand, Caz. *This Is Me, Full Stop.: The Art, Pleasures and Playfulness of Punctuation*. London: Particular Books, 2017.

Driver, Ann. *Music and Movement,* London: Oxford University Press, 1973.

Kinthissa. *Turning Silk: A Diary of Chen Taija Practice, the Quan of Change*. Oxford: Lunival, 2009.

Lecoq, Jacques, Carasso, J-G. and Lallias, J-C. *The Moving Body: Teaching Creative Theatre*. London: Routledge, 2001.

MacLennan, D. G. *Highland and Traditional Scottish Dances*. Edinburgh: W. T. McDougall, 1950.

McEvenue, Kelly. *The Alexander Technique for Actors*. London: Methuen, 2001.

Newlove, Jean. *Laban for Actors and Dancers: Putting Laban's Movement Theory into Practice, A Step-by-Step Guide*. London: Nick Hern Books, 2007.

Pisk, Litz. *The Actor and His Body*. London: Harrap, 1975.

Quirey, Belinda. *May I Have the Pleasure: The Story of Popular Dancing*. London: Dance Books Ltd, 1993.

Rodenburg, Patsy. *The Right To Speak: Working with the Voice*. London: Methuen, 1993.

Sabatine, Jean. *Movement Training for the Stage and Screen*. London: A & C Black, 1995.

Saint-Denis, Michel. *Theatre: The Rediscovery of Style*. London: Heinemann, 1960.

Smithson, Alison and Smithson, Peter. *Obras y proyectos Works and Projects*. Barcelona: Editorial Gustavo Gili, 2005.

Snow, Jackie. *Movement Training for Actors*. London: Methuen, 2012.

Tufnell, Miranda and Crickmay, Chris. *A Widening Field: Journeys in body and imagination*. Alton: Dance Books Ltd, 2004.

Tufnell, Miranda and Crickmay, Chris. *Body Space Image: Notes towards Improvisation and Performance*. Alton: Dance Books Ltd, 1993.

Van Der Kolk, Bessel. *The Body Keeps the Score: Mind, Brain and Body in the Transformation of Trauma*. London: Penguin, 2015.

Index

Page numbers in *italics* refer to illustrations.